Johannes Heinrich Hermann Gunkel
November 18, 1912

The Stories of Genesis

The Stories of Genesis

by

Hermann Gunkel

A translation of the third edition of the introduction to
Hermann Gunkel's commentary on the book of Genesis

Translated by John J. Scullion

Edited by William R. Scott

BIBAL Press
Publishing agency of BIBAL Corporation
Berkeley Institute of Biblical Archaeology & Literature

The Stories of Genesis

Library of Congress Cataloging-in-Publication Data

Gunkel, Hermann, 1862-1932.
  [Sagen der Genesis. English]
  The Stories of Genesis / by Hermann Gunkel ; translated by John J. Scullion ; edited by William R. Scott.
      p. cm.
  Translation of: Die Sagen der Genesis.
  "A translation of the third edition (1910) of the introduction to Hermann Gunkel's commentary on the book of Genesis."
  Includes index.
  ISBN 0-941037-29-0 : $34.95
  ISBN 0-941037-21-5 (pbk.) : $15.95
  1. Bible. O.T. Genesis--Criticism, interpretation, etc. 2. Bible. O.T. Genesis--Criticism, Form. I. Scullion, John. II. Scott, William R. (William Raymond), 1942-   . III. Title
BS1235.G8 1994
222'.11066--dc20   93-41722
                                                                         CIP
Published by BIBAL Press
P. O. Box 4531
Vallejo, CA 94590

                Printed at GRT Book Printing, Oakland, CA
                    Cover by KC Scott, Ashfield, MA
          Frontispiece courtesy of Prof. Dr. Rudolf Smend, D.D.

CONTENTS

Publisher's Foreword vii
Editor's Foreword ix
Translator's Foreword xiii
Translator's Introduction xv
Abbreviations xix

1. **Genesis is a Collection of Stories**
   History and Story 1
   Religion and Story 6
   Poetry and Story 7
2. **The Types of Stories in Genesis**
   God and People in the Stories 9
   Myth in Genesis 10
   Israel Reflects 11
   The Patriarchal Stories 13
   The Period when the Stories Originated 17
   Stories and Motifs: Historical, Ethnographic,
       Etiological, Ethnological, Etymological, Cultic 18
   The Mingling of Motifs 24
3. **The Artistic Form of the Stories in Genesis**
   Rhythm and Style in Biblical Story 27
   Story in Oral Tradition 29
   Units in Story 31
   The Length and the Arrangement of the Story 33
   The Number of Characters in the Story 35
   Principal and Secondary Characters 38
   Characterization 38
   Character Development 42
   Speech and Action in the Stories 45
   Attendant Circumstances in the Stories 48
   The Narrative Thread 49
   The Course of the Narrative 51
   The Art of the Story-Teller 53
   Compositional Style, Cycles of Stories 57
   The Age of the Narrative Style 62

CONTENTS

4. The History of the Transmission of the Stories in Oral Tradition
The Origins of the Stories 63
The Idea of God in the Stories 64
Yahweh 65
Foreign Influences 65
Foreign Parallels 69
Adaptation of Foreign Material 71
Convergence of Traditions 72
The Passage of the Stories through Time 73
The End of the Transmission 76
The Religion of Genesis and the Religion of Israel 77
Cult Stories 79
God and the Individual 80
The Stories and Morality 83
The Spirit and Flavor of the Stories 86
Stories: How Old and Late? 87
The Names in the Patriarchal Stories 88
The Patriarchs and Myth 90
The Patriarchs and History 91

5. Yahwist, Elohist, Jehovist, The Older Collections
Collectors and Writers 93
Sources and their Tributaries 94
The Collectors and their Material 98
The Schools of J and E 100
The Age of J and E 101
The Writing Down of the Stories 104

6. The Priestly Code and the Final Redaction
The Source P and its Characteristics 109
The Material in P 110
P, God, Religion and Morality 112
P and the Tradition 114
The Era of P 115
The Final Redactor 117
Genesis and Moses 118
Conclusion 119

Hermann Gunkel:
Biographical Data 121
Contributions to Biblical Scholarship 125
Indices 143

PUBLISHER'S FOREWORD

It seems appropriate to begin *The Stories of Genesis* by telling, in brief, the story behind the book. The last time I saw John Scullion, S.J., was on Wednesday, August 9, 1989, at the closing banquet of the international meeting of the Society of Biblical Literature in Copenhagen. We sat next to each other that delightful evening in the Store Festsal of the Moltkes Palæ and spent much of our time together discussing his desire to publish an English translation of the introduction to the third edition of Hermann Gunkel's commentary on Genesis. I recognized the significance of the project and asked him if he would be willing to have BIBAL Press take on the task. In the weeks that followed we reached a contractual agreement, in which Professor Scullion agreed to designate the royalties from the sale of this book to our "Translation and Publication Fund." The first announcement of the new "publication in process" appeared in the June 1990 issue of our newsletter, *The Armchair Archaeologist*; and then the project tragically stalled, almost indefinitely, when John Scullion died on November 24, 1990.

When Dr. William R. Scott took over as Director of BIBAL Press in May 1993, it soon became evident that the time had come to see the project through to completion. I take this opportunity to express my profound gratitude to him for his work in editing this volume. Because of the untimely death of John Scullion, his task was a demanding one and the end result is one for which he can be justly proud. He has transformed Scullion's unfinished manuscript into an invaluable reference work on Gunkel himself, including the "genesis" of Gunkel's thoughts on Genesis. We believe that this volume will remain in print for years to come as a substantial contribution to biblical scholarship.

We would also like to express our thanks to Professors Norbert Lohfink, S.J., and Ronald Clements for their part in making this publication possible by donating royalties from their publications with BIBAL Press into what we have now designated **The John Scullion Translation Fund**. Thus it is fitting that the first official publication of this fund should be *The Stories of Genesis*, which we dedicate as a memorial to John Scullion, S.J., one of the world's premier translators of German biblical scholarship.

Duane L. Christensen
President, BIBAL Corporation

EDITOR'S FOREWORD

John Scullion, S.J. passed away on November 24, 1990 while his translation of the introduction to the third edition of Gunkel's commentary on Genesis was still in a preliminary stage. After an interval of nearly three years, the task fell to me to complete this work and I can only hope that my efforts have done credit to the memory of a respected scholar.

Scullion was adamant that the German *Sage* in Gunkel's work should be translated as "story." His arguments are forceful (see his introduction) and I have not tampered with that decision. It does, however, introduce a significant problem for faithful translation in that Gunkel uses *Geschichte* in several ways, some of which must also be translated as "story." At the outset of this project I believed that the difference between *Sage* = story and *Geschichte* = story was important enough that the reader should be alerted by parenthetic notations. Indeed, Gunkel at times appears to use *Geschichte* as a generic designation of story and *Sage* as a more precise technical term. However, at other times he employs the two interchangeably, as on page 71 where he mentions that "individual stories (*Sagen*) stubbornly resisted Israelite adaptation" and cites as an example the *Peºnu'elgeschichte*. Much of the editing that Gunkel did for the third edition involved terminology; however, the reasons for his changes are not always clear. For instance, on p. 53 the first edition read "the creation story (*Geschichte*) is no *Sage*. He has changed this in the third edition to "the creation narrative (*Erzählung*) is no story (*Geschichte*). In spite of his caution that we should not refer to the creation narrative as story, he himself does so in subsequent portions of the introduction. Ultimately, I have concluded that Gunkel was not as precise in his terminology as we might wish and so have abandoned any effort to reveal such nuances in the translation. Readers who desire to explore Gunkel's terminology are cautioned to consult the original German.

The chapter division and titles are Gunkel's, but the subdivisions are either Scullion's (mostly) or mine. Gunkel numbered some paragraphs, but provided no subtitles for them. Our division is driven by what appear to be logical changes in content and does not in any way conform to Gunkel's. Several of our subdivisions actually occur in the middle of Gunkel's pages-long paragraphs.

Many of Gunkel's sometimes lengthy footnotes cite and pass judgment on now obscure works without contributing to his argument. Only those which either Scullion or I believe will be of interest to modern readers have been retained. These are printed in the text within brackets. In addition to footnotes, Gunkel also documented his work with parenthetical references in the text. Nearly all of these have been preserved and are placed inside parentheses.

I have rendered proper names found in the Bible according to the standards of the NRSV. Transliterations are either trans-literations according to modern custom of forms printed in Hebrew in the original or else faithfully reproduce Gunkel's own trans-literations except that *yod* has been rendered as "y" rather than the characteristic German "j."

I have, of course, made no attempt to conceal the fact that Gunkel proffers racial stereotypes in a manner that I would hope is objectionable to modern readers. However, this should be understood within the context of Gunkel's time and social setting. There are several indications that he may have been more aware of the implications of racial prejudice than many of his contemporaries. For instance, on page 85 he replaced the notion that people in Israel act stereotypically, which appeared in the first edition, with the general statement that "people" do so. Likewise, on page 86 he took some pains to put ancient Israelite stories in a favorable light in comparison to old German stories.

On the other hand, I did take the liberty of eliminating Gunkel's androcentric use of masculine pronouns to refer to people in general. In most cases it is clear that he did not mean to exclude women, and was only using the conventions of his time. But in order to maintain some consistency I have done this even where I suspect that he conceived of the individual or class as necessarily male as with, for example, the ancient storytellers. No change was made, however, to his use of masculine pronouns in reference to God, as I believe that to do so would inappropriately disguise the original tone of the work.

The differences between the first and third editions are considerable. As Gunkel himself pointed out in the preface to his third edition, hardly a page has been untouched and a great deal was added. To aid readers who might wish to compare these two editions, vertical lines have been placed in the outside margins to indicate material that has been relocated, added to or altered from that of the first edition. Triangular arrows point in toward places where material has been deleted, but no other changes made. These marginal notations have been provided only in cases which the editor judged to be significant. Minor word changes which do not alter the fundamental meaning and similar incidental editing have not been annotated.

The marginal annotations reflect differences between the German of the first (1901) edition of *Handkommentar zum alten Testament* (HKAT), published by Vandenhoeck & Ruprecht in Göttingen, and the German of the third (1910) edition of HKAT. Carruth's translation, first published in 1901 and reprinted in 1964, is an "elaborated" translation from the first edition of HKAT. It includes translation of a few phrases and sentences which did not appear in HKAT until the second edition in 1902. Thus an alert reader will notice that in a few cases there is no substantial difference between the two English translations, even though the marginal annotations indicate that there is a difference between the first and third German editions.

Much of Gunkel's editing was stylistic, involving only the substitution of synonyms. Hundreds of these appear to have been motivated by a desire to purge the work of the numerous foreign words which permeated the first edition. For instance, *Instrument* was replaced with *Werkzeug*, "ca." with *etwa*, *Etymologie* with *Namenserklärung*, *Tradition* with *Uberlieferung*, *Genre* with *Gattung*, etc. However, these replacements were not done consistently and Gunkel's editing often appears hurried, sometimes consisting of the addition of parenthetical statements that hang in disconcerting isolation from their immediate context. In other places, deletions have eliminated the referent of a subsequent demonstrative. In his preface, he also offered a blanket apology for contradictions which he knew he had created between the commentary and the new introduction. It is clear that he was driven more by the need to preserve all of his latest thinking than by a desire to produce a perfectly polished work.

With this in mind, it appears that his editing aimed at accomplishing four major goals. First, he radically changed and significantly enlarged the body of evidence, both biblical and extrabiblical, which he offered in support of his conclusions. By so doing, he considerably improved the forcefulness and credibility of many of his arguments. Second, he acknowledged research that had been published since the first edition and responded to criticism of his work. He appears to have been particularly anxious to avoid the impression that his work precluded treatment of Genesis as scripture and left no room for the guiding hand of God. This concern is clearly evident in the concluding paragraph, which is entirely new to the third edition. Third, he toned down many of his assertions by adding qualifiers such as "perhaps," "probably," "in general," etc. Finally, he updated some of his concepts and conclusions. The most striking example of this is that in the first edition, he conceived of a linear progression: *Mythos* → *Märchen* → *Sage*. Throughout the third edition, however, he assumes that *Märchen* came first and that both *Mythos* and *Sage* developed from it (see Scullion's discussion, pp. 136-7). Among others, there are also important differences in his sequence of transmission of the stories in Israel (p. 69) and in his views on the names of the patriarchs and the relationship of the patriarchal narratives to myth, particularly on whether or not the patriarchs are to be seen as former gods (pp. 88-92).

I would like to express my thanks to Norbert Lohfink and Ronald Clements who provided financial support for this project and to Susan Koeker for proofreading the manuscript. Finally, I would like to extend a special word of gratitude to Prof. Dr. Rudolf Smend of Georg-August-Universität in Göttingen, who graciously entrusted into our care his only original photograph of Hermann Gunkel. This photograph has been reproduced as the frontispiece.

William R. Scott
Fairfield, CA

TRANSLATOR'S FOREWORD

Hermann Gunkel's *Genesis* appeared in 1901. A third and thoroughly revised edition appeared in 1910. This edition was reprinted several times without alteration and appeared in a sixth and a seventh edition in 1964 and 1965 with an address by Walter Baumgartner to the Fourth Congress of the International Organization for the Study of the Old Testament held in Bonn, 1962, commemorating the centenary of Gunkel's birth.

The introduction to the first edition carried the title, "Die Sagen der Genesis" and covered seventy-one pages. It also appeared as a monograph with the same title from the publishers of the commentary (Vandenhoeck & Rupprecht, Göttingen). This introduction was translated into English by W.S. Carruth, *The Legends of Genesis* (Chicago: Open Court Press, 1901). Carruth's translation was reprinted as *The Legends of Genesis: The Biblical Saga and History* with an introduction by W.F. Albright (New York: Schocken Books, 1964. Listed in Schocken Books for reprinting, 1983-84).

The introduction to the third edition covered ninety-four pages. The present translation is of this third edition as represented in the sixth and seventh editions of 1964 and 1965. A ninth printing appeared in 1977.

A number of Gunkel's footnotes have been omitted; others have been modified; all that have been retained have been incorporated into the text.

I thank Dr. John S. Martin of the Department of Germanic Studies, University of Melbourne, and my colleague, Fr. Brian Moore, S.J., who read the translation and made useful suggestions. I also thank Mrs. Leonie Hudson who produced a manuscript of her usual very high standard.

John J. Scullion S.J.
Newman College
University of Melbourne

TRANSLATOR'S INTRODUCTION

Hermann Gunkel (1862-1932) was one of the most influential and learned Old Testament scholars of the 19th and 20th centuries. His contributions to biblical scholarship continued unbroken through the whole of his academic life, from the early works as a Privatdozent in Halle in the 1890's, to his final work as Professor and Professor Emeritus in the same city until his death on March 11, 1932. Throughout, he affirmed the obligation of Old Testament scholars to familiarize themselves with the history, culture, and literature of the Ancient Near East, and himself led the way. He was, of course, the pioneer in the area of form criticism. In his commentary on Genesis he investigated oral tradition as a living source of biblical tradition [cf. review of the 6th. ed. of *Genesis* by John L. McKenzie, *CBQ*, 25 (1964):487-488]. He also brought order into the study of the Psalms by classifying them according to types, and determined that most of them were set within the worshiping life of Israel in the period of the monarchy.

In the first edition of *Genesis* (1901), Gunkel traced a direct path from *Mythos* through *Märchen*. The former term means "myth," but for Gunkel, myth was simply "a story about the gods." At that time he regarded these as primal. The latter term means "story" or "folk story" (see below for a discussion of terms). In the third edition (1910) Gunkel came to the conclusion that *Märchen* was primal, and that *Mythos* and *Sage* developed from it. He was convinced that there was a rich *Märchen* or folklore tradition in Israel. Many of these motifs, however, "are simply elements from the world picture current at the time, or from myths of the surrounding world" [H.-J. Hermisson, *Enzyklopädie des Märchens*, 1, 1977, pp. 419-441].

The first edition carried scarcely a reference to literature in general or to literary critics in the field of *Germanistik* (the study of German language, literature, and history of literature). The third edition has a number of such references. Gunkel saw his own approach to folk story confirmed by Axel Olrik's influential essay,

"Epic Laws of Folk Narrative" [Danish, 1908; German 1909; English in Alan Dundes, ed., *The Study of Folklore*, (Englewood Cliffs, NJ: Prentice-Hall, 1965), pp.129-141]. Gunkel did not directly or consciously take over a method from *Germanistik*. He did, however, receive stimulus from the Grimm brothers (Jakob, 1785-1863, Wilhelm, 1786-1859) and was in debt to both Johann Wolfgang Goethe (1749-1832), and to Johann Gottfried Herder (1744-1803) — especially to Herder's *Vom Geist der hebräischen Poesie*, 1782-83. They were the leading figures coming out of the *Sturm und Drang* movement of the second half of the 18th century which freed the German *Geist* from the confinement of French classicism. [*Sturm und Drang* was the name of a play by Friedrich Maximilian Klinger, 1752-1831. The movement was at its height from 1765 to 1785.] But it was Gunkel alone who worked out his theory of the history of literature, literary forms, and story as applied to the Bible, though under the influence of Herder's "esthetic contemplation."

Gunkel confronted the problem of *Sage* in the Old Testament. *Sage* means story, folk story, popular story. It is not the equivalent of the English "saga," with which it has nothing to do. To translate it as "saga" is very misleading. Nor is "legend" an adequate rendering (see descriptions of terms below).

Gunkel entitled his introduction "Die Sagen der Genesis" ("The Stories of Genesis"). He gave the first chapter the title "Die Genesis ist eine Sammlung von Sagen" ("Genesis is a Collection of Stories"). His emphasis here was on "collection." The editors were collectors rather than redactors; they were more subject to the stories than were the stories to them, more servants of the material than its masters. One of Gunkel's chief aims was to grasp the religious meaning of the Old Testament by means of the *Sagen*. While he was grappling with this problem, he discovered that with the *Sage* one is dealing with a poetic genre. "Story (*Sage*) is popular, poetic narrative handed down from of old, dealing with people or events of the past. The word is used here solely in this generally acknowledged meaning."

Gunkel, of course, is not beyond criticism. His theories and explanations have been modified, but his basic insights were correct. Some recent criticisms and assessments of his work may be found in John H. Hayes, *An Introduction to the Old Testament*, pp. 121-154,

254-260, 286-305 (Nashville: Abingdon, 1979); in P. Gibert, *Une théorie de la légende: Hermann Gunkel et les légendes de la Bible*, esp. pp. 179-194 (Paris: Flammarion, 1979); and in John Van Seters, *In Search of History*, p. 38, and see index under Gunkel (New Haven: Yale University, 1983).

Märchen, Sage, Legende, Saga, Mythos

Märchen. This term suggests tale, folk tale, fairy tale, or tale of magic. It is indefinite as to time and place. In it the "unreal," i.e., the supernatural or preternatural, is normal. Animals and trees speak; people, fairy-godmothers and wizards appear and disappear; poor young men conquer monsters or overcome other obstacles to marry princesses; "and they lived happily ever after." There are no *Märchen* as such in the Old Testament, though there are *Märchen* motifs; e.g., the talking snake (Gen 3:1-7), Moses' staff changing from staff to serpent to staff (Exod 4:1-4; 7:8-13), Balaam's speaking ass (Num 22:28-30), Elijah's mantle (2 Kgs 2:8), and Elisha's floating iron axe head (2 Kgs 6:3-7).

Sage. This means story, popular story, or folk story. In it the real and the unreal worlds, the material and the supernatural, are quite distinct. There are devils and ghosts, dwarfs and giants, ogres and spirits. The folk story is rooted in the reality of the distant past, but has been worked over by poetic imagination in the process of transmission. There are many such folk tales in the Bible. *Sage* is not "saga" and it is an error to render it thus in English (see below under *Saga*). "The failure to understand that the German *Sage* means 'folk tale' or the like and has nothing to do with English 'saga' or its Icelandic original has misled generations and deprived form criticism of a valuable world" [D.J. McCarthy, *Treaty and Covenant*, p. 8 (Rome, 1981)].

Legende. Though in popular language legend is the virtual equivalent of "untrue," it should nevertheless in literary and biblical circles retain its well established, century old and current scholarly meaning of "a story about a holy person to be read to a community for its edification." French has but one word to render the German *Sage* and *Legende*, namely *légende*; hence a very useful and clear distinction is made between *légende populaire* (or *folklorique*) and *légende hagiographique*. From the seventeenth century, legend took on a transferred meaning of "an unauthentic story handed down by tradition and popularly regarded as unhistorical." In popular speech today, legend is a story of dubious veracity about historical persons or events. [There is some overlap between *Märchen* and *Sage*, and a great deal between *Sage* and *Legende*; cf. J. J. Scullion, "Märchen, Sage, Legende: Towards a Clarification of some Literary Terms Used by Old Testament Scholars," *VT* 34 (1984):321-336.]

Saga. The events related in the Icelandic sagas belong mainly to the period 874-1030 CE; and the sagas themselves were written down in the 13th century. It is for specialists to discuss whether the sagas were handed down in oral tradition and committed to writing in the later period, or were due to a flowering of creative writing in the 12th and 13th centuries. The Icelandic *segja* means "to tell" — something told by one to another. In modern Icelandic, *saga* includes both German *Historie* and *Geschichte*. Aage Bentzen has noted that the Swedish term "saga," used for the "chimerical fairy tale," is "not to be confounded with the usage in Danish-Norwegian-Icelandic, where this word denotes a 'history-narrative'" [*Introduction to the Old Testament*, p. 240, n. 3 (Copenhagen, 1948)]. The events narrated in the Norwegian and Icelandic sagas were *Historie*, that which actually happened; they became famed in *Geschichte*.

Mythos. "A definition of myth for the purpose of Old Testament study would not be built upon universal theoretical considerations, or even upon the universal phenomenology of religion at all times and in all places. Definition would begin from example. Thus we could say, 'By myth we mean, in this context, the sort of thing we find in Ugarit, or in Enuma Elish, or in other expressions of culture which in fact impinged on Israel with some directness.' We would thus leave for the moment undecided whether in fact such myth universally existed, or whether other types existed elsewhere which would also within their own sphere of relevance require to be designated myth" [James Barr, "The Meaning of 'Mythology'" *VT* 9 (1959):1-10]. One should not force on the Bible or the ancient Near East a sophisticated and abstract sociological, philosophical, psychological, or anthropological system of myth and pattern worked out in European culture in the 19th and 20th centuries.

ABBREVIATIONS

A.T.	Das Alte Testament (the Old Testament)
BZAW	Beihefte zur *Zeitschrift für die altestamentliche Wissenschaft*
comm.	Gunkel's commentary on Genesis, 3rd edition of HKAT
E	The Elohist source
Ed.	Editor
FRLANT	Forschungen zur Religion und Literatur des Alten und Neuen Testaments
HKAT	Handkommentar zum Alten Testament
J	The Yahwist source
NT	New Testament
OT	Old Testament
P	The Priestly source
PN	Personal name (substitutes for name of any person)
RGG	*Die Religion in Geschichte und Gegenwart*
SuC	*Schöpfung und Chaos in Urzeit und Endzeit*
VT	*Vetus Testamentum*
VTSup	Supplements to *Vetus Testamentum*
ZAW	*Zeitschrift für die altestamentliche Wissenschaft*
ZTK	*Zeitschrift für Theologie und Kirche*

Marginal Notations

Vertical lines in the outside margins indicate material in the third edition of HKAT that has been relocated, added to or altered from that of the first edition.

Triangular arrows in the outside margins point toward places where material which was in the first edition of HKAT has been deleted, but no other changes made.

1
GENESIS IS A COLLECTION OF STORIES

History and Story

Does Genesis (known as "The First Book of Moses") narrate history or story? For historians this is no longer a question. Nevertheless it is worthwhile stating clearly the reasons for their modern attitude.

History writing is not an art inborn in the human spirit. It had its origin at a definite stage of development in the course of human history. Uncultivated peoples do not write history. They do not have the capacity to reproduce their experiences objectively, and they have no interest in passing on to posterity an accurate account of the events of their time. Their experiences fade unnoticed and reality mingles with fantasy. They can express historical events only in poetic form, in songs and stories.

It is only at a certain level of civilization, when objectivity has developed sufficiently and the urge to communicate one's own experiences to posterity has become strong enough, that history writing can begin. Its subject is great public events—the deeds of leaders of peoples and of kings, especially wars. History writing therefore presupposes some sort of political organization. Later (in most cases much later) the art of history writing, which the human race learned from writing political history, was transferred to other areas, and hence gave rise to memoirs or family history. But there are large groups of people which have never risen to history in the strict sense, and have remained permanently on the level of story (or its modern analogies).

We find then in ancient civilizations two different types of historical transmission: history writing in the strict sense and, side by side with it, popular tradition which deals partly with the same material, but in popular and imaginative ways, and relates partly to

1

the ancient prehistorical period. Such popular transmissions can also preserve historical recollections, even though in poetic form.

The rise of history writing in Israel was no different. In the period that passed Genesis on to us, Israel had already long known history writing, in a highly developed form by the standard of the time, which dealt with the deeds of kings and especially with wars. The narratives of what are known as the two books of Samuel are in particular a monument to this [see my article "Geschichtsschreibung" in A.T., *RGG*]. But in a people like Israel, so poetically endowed, story too has had its place. Because "story" was misunderstood and interchanged with "lie," one had reservations about accepting it in the Old Testament. But story is not lie; it is rather a particular type of poetical writing. *Story is popular poetic narrative, handed down from of old, dealing with people or events of the past.* The word is used here solely in this generally acknowledged meaning. If the lofty spirit of the Old Testament makes use of so many poetic forms, why not of this? Rather, as with every religion, the religion of Israel cherished poetry and poetic narrative. Poetic narrative is much better suited than simple prose to convey ideas—particularly religious ideas: "Stories are incomparably deeper, freer and truer than chronicles and histories; what would the longest and most trustworthy chronicles of all the Burgundian kings be in comparison with *Siegfried and Kriemhild*"? [F. Paulsen, *Deutsche Schule*, 1901, p. 139.] Genesis is much more a religious book than are the books of Kings.

It is certain that there are stories in the Old Testament—one has only to think of Samson and of Jonah. It is not a question here of belief or unbelief, but simply of a better perception of whether the narratives of Genesis are history or story.

One counters by saying that Jesus and the apostles clearly held these narratives to be reality and not poetry. Certainly. But the men of the New Testament have no special standing in this matter; they shared the opinions of their time. We ought not look for a solution to this question in the New Testament.

Inasmuch as story and history are very different in origin and kind, there are many criteria by which they can be distinguished. One of the most important is that story usually originates and is transmitted in oral tradition, whereas history takes written form. The reason for this lies in the nature of the two genres. Story is the way of transmission of preliterate groups; history belongs to the scholarly occupations and presupposes the skill of writing. At the same time writing serves to fix a tradition. Oral tradition cannot in the long run preserve itself intact and so has not the capacity to be an adequate vessel for history.

Now it is obvious that Genesis contains the final distillation in writing of oral tradition. The patriarchal narratives show no sign at all that the patriarchs themselves wanted to have them written down. Rather, there are many passages which show clearly the long lapse of time between the patriarchal period and the narrators ("to this day," Gen 19:38; the list of the kings of Edom up to David, Gen 36:31ff; the sentence, "at that time the Canaanites were in the land," Gen 12:6; 13:7, must have been written when this people had long since disappeared). The whole style of the narratives is comprehensible only under the presupposition of their oral transmission, as will be shown in chapter 3. This fact is obvious from the many variants which will be dealt with below (chapter 4). If Genesis contains oral tradition about remote antiquity, then, according to what has been said above, it is also story.

A further distinguishing criterion is the circle in which story and history move. Great public events are the real subject of history; the historian only speaks of private matters in so far as they are of significance for public affairs. Story, however, talks of those things which are of interest to people, of the personal and the private, and likes to interpret even political events and personalities so as to give them a popular interest. History has to narrate how and for what reasons David succeeded in freeing Israel from the Philistines. Story prefers to narrate how the boy David slew a Philistine giant. Which of these is characteristic of the material of Genesis? With the single exception of chapter 14, there is not a word about great political events. The subject matter is not the history of kings and princes; it is predominantly the history of a private family. We hear of a host of details which, whether attested or not, are for the most part without any value for real (political) history: Abraham was pious and magnanimous. He expelled his concubine to please his wife. Jacob tricked his brother. Rachel and Leah were jealous of each other. These are "insignificant anecdotes from agricultural life, stories about wells, watering places and the bed-chamber" [Ed. — no source cited]. They make pleasant reading but are not historical events. The historian does not report these things, but popular tradition delights in them as it passes on the story. Furthermore, when Abraham put all his trust in God, or when Jacob buried foreign gods at Shechem, or the like, these events aroused no public attention when they took place.

For every account that claims to be a trustworthy historical recollection, one must be able to conceive of a path which leads from the eyewitnesses of the event reported down to the reporter. It is different for story, which is the result partly of transmission, partly of imagination. One needs only to apply this measure to the early narratives of Genesis in order to recognize their character immediately. No one was present at creation. No human line of transmission stretches back to the origin of our race, to primal peoples, to primal languages. In earlier times, before the decipherment of the Egyptian and Babylonian records, Israelite tradition could appear so ancient that it seemed not impossible to find in it recollections of these prehistoric ages. But now, with our world view so enormously broadened, when we see that the people of Israel was one of the youngest among its neighbors, such conjectures are definitively at an end. Millennia passed between the origin of the first peoples of the Near East and the appearance of the people of Israel. There can be no serious talk of historical traditions which Israel may have had about those primeval times.

There must be the gravest reservations too about the patriarchal narratives. According to the tradition, four hundred years elapsed after the patriarchal period, during which Israel was living in Egypt. Nothing is narrated from this period. Apart from a few genealogies, the historical memory must have been completely obliterated. Yet a wealth of insignificant details is narrated about the patriarchal period. How is it conceivable for a people to preserve such minute details from the history of its ancestors? Oral tradition is not capable of retaining with complete fidelity details of this kind in all their freshness through so long a period. One has only to look at the narratives in detail. In most cases one cannot even put the question—"How could the reporter know the things which are narrated?"—without provoking laughter. How could the narrator of the flood story claim to know how much water there was? Would Noah have measured it? How could one have known what God alone in heaven or in the heavenly council said or thought (Genesis 1; 2:18; 6:3, 6-7; 11:6-7)?

The most obvious characteristic of story is that it often reports things which to us are beyond belief. The verisimilitude of this sort of poetry is different from that of everyday life, and ancient Israel held much to be possible which we think impossible. Many things are reported in Genesis which contradict our better knowledge. We know that there are many more species of animals than could fit into the ark; that Ararat is not the highest mountain in the world; that the firmament of heaven, about which the creation story in Gen 1:6ff speaks, is not real but an optical illusion; that the stars cannot possibly have come into being after the plants, as Genesis narrates; that the streams of the earth do not for the most part take their origin from the four main rivers, as Gen 2:10-14 says; that the Euphrates and the Tigris have not the same source; that the Dead Sea had been there long before people lived in Palestine and did not have its origin in historical times, as Gen 14:3 thinks; that a period of only 2666 years from creation to the exodus of Israel from Egypt is quite impossible, not only according to the discoveries of geology, but also according to the historical documents of the Babylonians and Egyptians, and so on.

Most of the explanations of names in Genesis cannot be accepted, as our scientific knowledge of language shows. Yet even primal names, and a word like Babel, are derived unhesitatingly from Hebrew under the presupposition, self-evident in ancient Israel but quite impossible in fact, that the earliest language of mankind was Hebrew.

The theory that underpins the stories of the fathers, namely that all peoples had their origin by propagation from one family, each stemming from one primeval father, is utterly childish (see chapter 2 below, and comm. on Gen 9:18-19; 10:1b, 8-19, 21, 25-30, the table of the nations according to J). Our modern historical view of the world, which is certainly not invented, but based on the observation of facts, tells us otherwise, and shows this to be impossible. And however reserved the modern historian may be in the face of what he or she holds to be impossible, one will at any rate be certain that animals—snakes and donkeys—do not talk, nor have they ever; that there is no tree whose fruit confers immortality or knowledge; that angels do not have bodily union with humans (Gen 6:1ff); that 318 men and some allies cannot rout a world power (Gen 14:14-15); and that no one can live 969 years (Gen 5:27). However, it is especially noteworthy that Hebrew narrative is not sensible to the great lack of verisimilitude in what is reported. The first woman was not surprised when the snake began to talk to her; the narrator did not ask how Noah managed to get the animals into the ark, and so on. This is a

clear indication that we would be doing an injustice to such simplicity
were we to align it with concrete reality.

Religion and Story

The narratives of Genesis are for the most part of a religious
kind, and so they constantly speak of God. But the way in which they
do so is one of the surest measures for determining whether they are
intended to be historical or poetic. Here too the historian does not
manage without a philosophical conception of the world. We believe
that God is at work in the world as the quiet, hidden background of
everything. Sometimes his action is tangible, especially in great and
impressive events and persons. We sense his rule in the wonderful
concatenation of things, but he never appears to us as an active agent
among others. He is always the ultimate cause of everything.

It is quite different in many narratives in Genesis. There God
strolled in the garden, formed humans with his own hands and closed
the door of the ark (Gen 7:16); he breathed into humans his own
breath and experimented unsuccessfully with the animals (Gen
2:19-20); he smelled Noah's sacrifice (Gen 8:21); he appeared to
Abraham and Lot in the form of a traveler (Genesis 18-19), or as an
angel called from heaven (Gen 22:11, and elsewhere). God appears
to Abraham once in a form peculiar to himself, looking like a flaming
torch and a smoking cooking pot (Gen 15:17)! It is characteristic of
Genesis that when God speaks, his words are not sensed in the dark
hours of deepest human excitation, in ecstasy; i.e., in the way God's
prophets heard his voice. Rather, God speaks simply as one person
to another. We are prepared to understand this as the naïveté of
ancient humans, but we refuse to believe in such narratives.

Such lines of argument are strengthened very markedly when
one compares these narratives, which we hold from internal reasons
to be poetry, with well known examples of Israelite history writing.
Such violations of verisimilitude — such impossibilities — do not occur
everywhere in the Old Testament, but only in quite specific passages
of similar nature. We do not observe them in passages which for
other reasons we hold to be strictly or more strictly historical. Take,
for example, the central passage of 2 Samuel, the story of the revolt
of Absalom, which is the most precious jewel of history writing in
Israel. The world described there is a world well known to us. There
no iron floats on water, no snake talks, neither God nor an angel

appears as one person among others. All happens in just the way to which we are accustomed. The distinction between story and history is not something introduced into the Old Testament from outside; it is there for the careful observer to discern.

Further, one should reflect that individual narratives in Genesis are not only similar to stories of other peoples, but are related to them in origin and type. One cannot maintain that the account of the flood in Genesis is history and that the Babylonian account of the flood is story. The Old Testament flood narrative is offspring and recension of the Babylonian. Nor can one explain all other narratives of the creation of the world as fantasy and Genesis 1 as history. Genesis 1, however much its religious spirit differs from that of other creation narratives, is very close to them in literary type.

Poetry and Story

However, what is and remains the main thing is the poetic tone of these narratives. History writing, which aims to inform about what really happened, is of its nature prose. But story is of its nature poetry. It is intended to give pleasure, to elevate, to inspire, to move. One who wants to do justice to such ancient narratives must have sufficient esthetic sense to be able to perceive, by listening to one of them, what it is and what it wants to be. It is therefore not a question of passing an unfavorable or indeed incredulous judgment, but rather of grasping with appreciation the nature of the thing. Whoever has heart and feeling must be aware, for example, that the story of the sacrifice of Isaac is not concerned with stating certain historical facts. Rather, the listener is meant to share the heart-rending agony of the father who is to sacrifice his own child with his own hand, and then his boundless gratitude and joy when God's grace remits this heavy burden. Whoever has appreciated the characteristic poetic charm of this ancient story is annoyed with the barbarian—and there are pious barbarians—who can only appreciate these narratives by seeing them as prose and history. The judgment that such a narrative is story ought by no means to detract from it. Rather, it ought to indicate that the one passing the judgment has experienced something of the narrative's poetic beauty, and believes that he or she has thus understood it. Only ignorance can consider such a judgment impious; rather, it is both pious and appreciative. These poetic narratives are certainly the most beautiful possession that a people brings along on its journey through history; and Israel's stories, especially the stories of Genesis, are perhaps the most beautiful and most profound ever known on earth.

A child, who cannot yet distinguish between reality and poetry, is somewhat upset when told that beautiful stories are "not true." But such an attitude would ill become a modern theologian. The Evangelical church and its official representatives would do well not to resist—as has hitherto so often happened—the stories that Genesis contains, but to grasp that without such scholarly knowledge a historical understanding of Genesis is impossible. This knowledge has now become too much a part of historical education to allow itself to be suppressed. It will certainly get through to our people; the process is irresistible. We are anxious that it be presented to them in the right spirit.

2
THE TYPES OF STORIES IN GENESIS

God and People in the Stories

Two groups of stories stand out clearly among the great mass of material in Genesis. The first group consists of stories about the origin of the world and the primal ancestors of the human race. This includes the stories up to the tower of Babel. The scene of these narratives is the distant past and their sphere of interest is the whole world. The second group consists of stories about the fathers of Israel — Abraham, Isaac, Jacob and their sons. Their setting is the land of Canaan and its environs; and interest is centered on one family, with the thought ever hovering with more or less clarity in the background that from it God's people is to come.

There is also a difference in the idea of God. In the primeval stories he is more universal. Yahweh is the creator of heaven and earth (Gen 2:4b; or at least of human beings and animals, Gen 2:5ff) and is the lord and judge of the human race (in the stories of the garden, the angel marriages, the flood, the building of the tower). But the god who appears in the patriarchal narratives, who visits Abraham and protects Jacob, who intervenes in the minor happenings of the life of the individual, who prospers the journey and provides for hospitality, seems more like a family god. To be sure, however, he is a god with whom the God of the people of Israel and the numen of the localities of Canaan are connected.

There are other differences as well. An aloof and baneful mood prevails in the primeval stories. They tell of fearful divine judgments and presuppose a deep gulf between the human race and the divinity which humans do not overstep with impunity. But in the patriarchal narratives there appears a god whose inviolable grace even watches over children and grandchildren. Furthermore, in the patriarchal stories the divinity is always there in secret, unnoticed, or simply

9

speaking from heaven, or just in a dream. But in the primeval stories the idea of God is more anthropomorphic. God moves intimately among people and no one is surprised at this. The story of the garden presupposes that God came to visit them every morning. He shut the door of the ark after Noah, and came to him in person, allured by his sacrifice. He even formed people and animals with his own hands, experimenting unsuccessfully. In the flood narrative he repented that he created human beings, and then at the end promised never again to inflict so horrible a punishment. In the story of the tower he seems for a moment to be almost afraid of the growing power of the human race, and so on.

The actors in the patriarchal stories are always people. If the divinity appears, it is by way of exception. But in the primeval stories it is the divinity who carries the action (in the creation) or is at least the main contributor (the garden, the angel marriages of Gen 6:1ff, the flood, the building of the tower). This difference is merely relative, because the divinity makes its appearance in certain patriarchal stories, such as the Hebron and Sodom narratives (Genesis 18-19), as well as in the Penuel episode (Gen 32:25ff). On the other hand people are the actors or main actors in the Cain and Abel story as well as in the cursing of Canaan. These too are to be numbered among the stories. The predominance of the activity of the divinity in the primeval stories means that these stories have a mythical stamp; they are faded myths.

Myth in Genesis

Myths — let no one be frightened of the word — are stories about the gods, differing from stories proper in which the actors are humans. Now the mythical narratives of Genesis have come to us in relatively faded colors. We perceive this from the narratives themselves because we are in a position, at certain points, to infer an older form than that handed down (comm. p. 9). For example, the present text of Gen 6:1-4 is but a torso (comm. p. 59). We also see this when we compare the primeval stories with the mythological references that we encounter in the Old Testament poets and prophets and in the later apocalyptic writers (comm. pp. 33ff, 120ff, and the material collected in *Schöpfung und Chaos*, 1895). We come to the same conclusion (and here it is very clear) when we compare the primeval stories with oriental myths, especially the biblical creation and flood stories with the Babylonian versions (comm. pp. 125ff, 67ff). The vast contours, the characteristically brilliant colors proper to these myths in their origin, have become blurred in the biblical accounts. These would include the equation of divine figures with natural objects or areas, the struggles between the gods, the begetting of gods, etc. — none of which is present in Genesis. It is here that one can discern what is characteristic of Israelite religion, namely that it was not favorable to myth. From the outset it was directed towards monotheism. But a history of the gods requires at least two divinities.

And so the Israel that we come to know in the Old Testament did not tolerate unadulterated myths, at least not in prose. Concessions to myth were, however, allowed to the poet. Poetry therefore preserves the remnants of a more ancient attitude, preceding the Genesis tradition. This older attitude came to terms with myth without embarrassment. The primeval stories preserved for us in Genesis, however, are dominated throughout by an unspoken reserve in the face of myth. The monotheism of Israel admits only of those myths in which either God acts alone (as in the creation account) or else in which the story takes place between God and humans. The former can not really be considered (hi)story since in (hi)story a third situation results from action and counteraction. As regards the latter, Israel's understanding was that humans are too weak to be worthy opponents of God and thus to enter into conflict with him on a major scale. As soon as God intervenes, all is decided. If one wants in such a case to narrate any (hi)story at all, then the initiative must come from below. This is what is done in the stories of the garden and the tower. The flood story is different since God appears in it at the very beginning. But as a consequence the listener is not drawn into any suspense about the fate of the human race.

One should further note that the stories handed down which have mythical echoes are far fewer in number than the patriarchal stories, where there is no mythical element. Here too one can perceive the effect of an aversion to myth.

Israel Reflects

Genesis has no pure myths of its own. Hence it is not necessary to enter into a detailed discussion here about the origins, type and primal meaning of myth. We can be content with the simple definition of myth as "a story about the gods" and with a few remarks relevant to Genesis.

There is a series of myths in which it is possible to recognize that the narrative of a primeval event has been colored by a similar phenomenon which occurs often (or else regularly) in the real world. The creation of the world, for example, is portrayed as a great springtime, and the frequent appearance of the rainbow after rain was the occasion of a narrative about its origin after the flood.

Many myths answer questions and teach. So it is with the primeval stories of Genesis. The creation story asks: Where do heaven and earth come from? Why is the sabbath holy? The garden narrative asks: Whence the human intellect and the fate of death? Whence the human body and spirit? Whence language? Whence the love between the sexes (Gen 2:24)? How is it that the woman experiences such pain in childbirth and that the man has to till the recalcitrant land or that the snake crawls on its belly? And so on. In these cases the answer to the question constitutes the intrinsic content of the story. It is different with the flood story which appears to reproduce a historical event (comm. p. 76). However the etiological element (giving the reason) is there at the end: Why doesn't the flood come again (Gen 8:21-22; 9:8ff)? What does the rainbow mean (Gen 9:12ff)? The natural conclusion of such a story is "and so." "And so a man leaves his father and his mother and cleaves to his wife" (Gen 2:24). But none of these questions is concerned with matters peculiar to Israel—and here myths differ specifically from stories in that myths are concerned with matters affecting the whole world.

We know that in general ancient Israel was not inclined to speculation. It was almost always preoccupied with the immediate and with what was Israelite. But here is a situation where this ancient people was in a position to deal with general human problems and with the most profound questions affecting the human race. This happened to a certain degree in the stories of the creation and the garden, which are the beginnings of theology and philosophy. It is no wonder that in the post-biblical period special emphasis has fallen on these passages, and that as long as Genesis has been read every generation up to the present day has read its most profound thoughts into these narratives.

A particular group of etiological narratives, which Gressmann calls "stories about civilization" [*ZAW* 30 (1910):25], inquires into the origin of human habits: how old is the practice of eating fruit and flesh or of clothing oneself with leaves and skins, and how did these customs originate? The same questions apply to cattle breeding, agriculture, the arts of metallurgy and music, city building and political life. Answers to these questions were proposed in the stories of the garden, of the Kenites and of the tower.

The Patriarchal Stories

The primeval stories are followed by the patriarchal stories. Their heroes are the tribal fathers or ancestors of the nations, particularly of Israel. Basic to these stories is the notion that each nation, and so Israel, took its origin from the family of one of the ancestors which then continually expanded. This notion found expression in Israel in the formula which in many (though not all) instances described the nation or people as "sons of PN." Such a theory was also current among the Arabs and was known to the Greeks, at least in the more ancient period. However, there is no trace of it in either Egypt or Babylon. A consequence of this concept is that relationships between peoples were explained by means of the family tree. Two peoples, it was said, had brothers as ancestors. This meant that the peoples were closely related and stood as equals. If one happened to be richer, stronger or nobler, this was explained by saying that its tribal ancestor was the firstborn brother, or that he descended from the better mother, and that the other was the younger, or was descended from the concubine. The division of Israel into twelve tribes was explained by conceiving the ancestor, Israel, as having had twelve sons. If some of the tribes were closely linked, then it was because they derived from the same mother. More distant relationships existed between the uncle and the nephew, Abraham and Lot, and between the ancestors of Israel on the one hand, and Moab and Ammon on the other.

There is something sound in this theory, inasmuch as the bond which forms the unity of the family or tribe in the simple relationships of desert peoples is not some sort of political organization but has the sense of blood relationship. Furthermore, many families do in fact descend from the male, or at least claim the one after whom they call themselves as their leader. On the other hand, we know enough about the origin of peoples and tribes to be able to say that they are also formed in quite different ways. For example, foreign groups may be assimilated or there may be a fusion of immigrants with residents. Israel's constantly vaunted purity of blood is a figment of the imagination.

Hence the theory that peoples generally take their origin from the family of a single ancestor proceeds not from observation of facts, but from mythical thinking which tried to comprehend everything—and so peoples—as arising from procreation. In any case, a numerous tribe or a whole people is too far removed in time from the tribal ancestor to whom it lays claim to be able to have any oral information about him. In cases where there is not only a family tree extant, but certain stories are also narrated about the ancestor, the explanation is that the experiences and circumstances of the people itself have been transferred to the primeval figure. This is perfectly obvious in many cases. When a person named Shechem, the ancestor of the city of Shechem, is described as a popular young man who was killed by Simeon and Levi, the ancestors of two tribes, everyone regards this not as history, but as historical experiences clothed in story. We are not distorting the stories or story fragments that deal with such tribal figures. On the contrary we only grasp their real meaning and make it accessible when we try to understand the heroes about whom they speak as peoples and tribes, and to explain the stories about them as being primarily the experiences of peoples.

However, one must proceed very cautiously here. We must reckon with the possibility that some of these figures did not originally represent peoples. It may have only been later tradition that subsequently elevated them to ancestor status. Furthermore, after the "ancestral" figures had become established as heroes in narratives, narratives of a different sort which did not have their origin in popular (tribal) history became attached to them. We can be sure that certain figures may be understood as personifications of peoples and tribes, particularly those whose names are known to us as names of peoples, e.g., Cain, Canaan, Ishmael, Ammon, Moab, the twelve tribes and their families. But it is different with figures like Abraham, Isaac, and Jacob, the ancestors of Israel; with Lot, the tribal ancestor of Ammon and Moab; with Esau, the tribal ancestor of Edom; and with Laban "the Aramaean." These figures do not bear the names of the peoples and tribes which they represent. They must have originally had another significance and were only elevated to become representatives of their peoples by the demands of tradition. Hence it follows that certain details narrated about them can go back to the historical development of their people, though all is not to be understood as a systematic account of what happened. One must proceed with even more reserve in the case of such figures as Abel and with the women: Sarah, Hagar, Rebekah, Leah, Rachel, Dinah, and Tamar. It is not at all clear that each of these is meant to represent a tribe. It is to be noted further that Shem, Ham and Japheth were perhaps primal peoples and that Jacob and Esau may have represented two groups of peoples (comm. p. 316). Many of the narratives which deal with the ancestors (and we speak cautiously here) originally portrayed the experiences of peoples.

We can suppose that in ancient times there were disputes about wells between the inhabitants of Gerar and the roving Bedouin until they finally made a treaty in Beer-sheba. The story describes these events as a dispute and treaty between Abimelech of Gerar and the ancestors Abraham and Isaac (Gen 21:22ff; 26). Simeon and Levi insidiously murdered the young Shechem, but Jacob dissociated himself from the brothers (Genesis 34). The history that gave rise to this would have been as follows. The Canaanite city of Shechem was treacherously overcome by the tribes of Simeon and Levi, but the other tribes of Israel remained neutral (cf. comm. p. 371). A part of the Tamar story, Genesis 38, describes the ancient situation of the tribe of Judah. In the story of Hirah, the Adullamite, and Judah's wife Shua, Judah co-operated with the Canaanites. A number of Judahite-Canaanite groups (Er and Onan) disappeared early and finally two new groups (Perez and Zerah) arose (comm. pp. 411-412, 418).

There are echoes of history—more precisely of the history of civilization in the broader sense—in the Jacob-Esau stories. We hear how the shepherd, though the younger brother, surpassed the hunter by his superior cleverness (comm. p. 316). The Cain-Abel story is comparable (comm. p. 48). The stories of the two Judahite families, Perez and Zerah (Gen 38:27ff) as well as of Ephraim and Manasseh (Gen 48:13-14) presuppose similar fraternal strife. The former perhaps, and the latter almost certainly, are to be understood as echoes of historical events. Reuben, the firstborn of the Israelite tribes, lost his rights as firstborn because of some crime (Gen 49:3-4). The tribe of Reuben, which had precedence in the most ancient period, has thus forfeited its position. Shem, Ham and Japheth were ◄ originally brothers; but Japheth now has a more extensive territory than the others, and Canaan must be a slave to both (Gen 9:20ff).

We often hear of migrations. Abraham migrated from the northeast to Canaan, as did Rebekah (to marry Isaac), and finally Jacob. The starting points of these migrations are described as Ur of the Chaldees, Haran (the city of Nahor, Gen 24:10-11), and the land of the "sons of the east." It is a matter of dispute how old this information is and whether it reflects historical events, though there is no compelling objection to the assertion that it does (comm. p. 168). The Joseph story, for example, presupposes a migration of Hebrew tribes to Egypt and the narrative of Abraham's journey down to Egypt contains the same motif (Gen 12:10ff).

It is the very nature of story that we do not perceive ancient events clearly in them, but rather as through a mist. The story has spun its poetic web over the historical reminiscences and obscured its outlines. The process of popular transmission has added all sorts of things to that which was their own. Thus figures of entirely different origins, as we have just seen, have coalesced to form ancestors; and the historical and the imaginative have been woven into the single, unified web which we now see. The result is that the period in which the event took place cannot for the most part be determined from the story. Often not even the place is certain, and now and again not even the matter at issue. Story has forgotten where Jacob and Esau, Cain, Shem and Japheth actually lived or what Jacob and Esau originally meant. The scholar who would derive historical events from stories needs to be urgently warned not to proceed pedantically, and not to surrender to the belief that it is possible to directly recover historical facts by simple retrojection into the popular history of peoples from the patriarchal stories (see below).

Although these stories might obscure rather than reveal the events of the past, only a barbarian would despise them for that reason. They are often more precious than straightforward prose accounts of what happened. For example, if we were to have an accurate historical account of Ishmael, we would remain more or less indifferent to it because this "wild ass" accomplished scarcely anything for the human race. But because an imaginative hand has painted him, he lives on forever.

The character of the tribes or groups described in these stories is clear. There is Esau, the hunter on the steppes who lived from hand to mouth without much forethought—forgetful, generous and courageous. There is Jacob, the shepherd, who was much cleverer and was careful to provide for the future. His uncle Laban is typical of the sheep breeder in the Near East, avaricious and deceitful, but outwardly of outstanding probity, never embarrassed by evasion. Ishmael, the Bedouin, is a "wild ass" of a man, and Cain slinks like a murderer far from Yahweh's blessed land.

In many cases the moods in which the events are conceived come through to us. We hear very clearly how the story despises Canaan's impurity, how it laughs at Esau and Laban, how it takes pleasure that Lot's greed gains only the poorer land, and so on.

The Period when the Stories Originated

Because these narratives are available to us from two sources (J and E) which come from somewhere in the 9th and 8th centuries, it has been commonly believed that the stories themselves originated in essence in the period of the Israelite monarchy and provide no information about history previous to this (cf. J. Wellhausen, *Prolegomena to the History of Ancient Israel*, Eng. 1957, pp. 318-319). In fact, however, they are much older. The names that occur in them attest to this; they have been almost entirely forgotten even when we can vouch for their historicity. We know nothing from the process of historical transmission in Israel about Shem, Ham, and Japheth, scarcely anything about Reuben, Simeon and Levi; and it is only the oldest (or older) transmission that tells us anything about Ishmael and Cain. These then are names of ancient peoples and tribes older than historical Israel. It is quite obvious that the stories of Jacob and Esau are very ancient. It is true that these figures were subsequently equated with Israel and Edom; however, the double names and a number of traits in the story which do not fit the historical peoples of Edom and Israel demonstrate that the old narrative had a very different situation in view. In the story, Jacob was in craven fear of his brother. Historically, Israel overcame Edom in war. In the story, Esau was stupid. Historically, he was famed for his wisdom (comm. p. 316).

We can advance another proof for the antiquity of such stories from the history of story in Israel. The stories in the book of Judges in general no longer speak of the ancestors of tribes or peoples (except Judges 1), but of individual tribal leaders. The last historically datable story which is colored by the old style is the story of the attack on Shechem – the Dinah story of Genesis 34. As far as we can see, therefore, this type of narrative disappeared in the

ancient period of the judges. From that time on such narratives were
still transmitted, but not created anew.

Stories and Motifs: Historical, Ethnographic Etiological, Ethnological, Etymological, Cultic

We call stories historical stories when they reflect historical
events and ethnographic stories when they portray predominantly the
status of peoples. The stories about the treaty at Beer-sheba, the
attack on Shechem, the dying out of the older Judahite tribes are
historical. The stories of Cain and of Ishmael are ethnographic.

Together with these motifs the Genesis narratives contain
etiological motifs, i.e., motifs whose purpose it is to explain
something (a motif in this sense is a basic, self-contained unit of
poetic material). There was an abundance of questions which might
▶ preoccupy an ancient people. The child looks wide-eyed at the world
and asks, "Why?" The answer that it gives and with which it is readily
content is perhaps quite childish and so quite wrong. Nevertheless, if
it is a well-disposed child, the answer is fascinating and stimulating,
even for adults. Ancient people raised such questions and answered
them as best they could. These questions were usually the same as
those we raise and try to answer in our scientific disciplines. We are
dealing here, then, with the beginnings of human science—very
modest beginnings to be sure, but beginnings which demand our
respect. This is particularly stimulating and attractive for us because
these answers articulate ancient Israel's most intimate impressions,
clothed in the colorful garment of poetry.

Some questions of this sort are ethnological. What are the
reasons for the relationships between peoples? Why is Canaan a
slave to its brothers? Why has Japheth so vast a territory (Gen
9:24ff)? Why do the sons of Lot dwell in the unproductive east
(comm. p. 176)? How was it that Reuben lost his right of primo-
geniture (Gen 49:3-4)? Why must Cain wander about homeless and
a fugitive? Why will sevenfold vengeance be taken on the one who
slays Cain? Why is Gilead the boundary facing the "sons of the east"
(Gen 31:52)? Why does Beer-sheba belong to us and not to the
people of Gerar (Gen 21:22ff; 26:25ff)? Why does Joseph own
▶ Shechem (Gen 48:22)? Why did Ishmael become a desert people
with this as its possession and with this God (Genesis 16)? Why is it
that the Egyptian peasants have to bear the heavy tax of one fifth of

their produce while the fields of the priests are free (Gen 47:13ff)? The question is very often raised: Why does Israel possess the beautiful land of Canaan? The stories narrate in a number of ways how the fathers acquired this land. God promised it to Abraham because of his obedience (Gen 12:7); when Lot chose the east at the parting at Bethel, the west became Abraham's property (Genesis 13); Jacob acquired the blessing of the better land from Isaac by trickery (Genesis 27); God promised it to Jacob at Bethel (Gen 28:13), and so on.

In individual cases it is often scarcely possible to distinguish between ethnological stories of this kind, which narrate a fictitious event in order to explain the relationship between peoples, and historical stories, which contain a fragment of a tradition of an event that really happened. Ethnological and ethnographic elements are usually found side by side in the same story. The relationships presupposed are historical, the way in which they are explained is poetic.

The answer given to these questions always follows the same line — explaining the present circumstances from something that the primal fathers have done. It was the primal ancestor who dug the well at Beer-sheba, and so it belongs to us, his heirs (Gen 26:25ff); the primal ancestors established Gilead as a boundary (Gen 31:52); Cain's tribal ancestor was cursed by God to eternal wandering, and so on. A favorite device is to find an explanation of something in an extraordinary oracle pronounced by God himself or by one of the fathers. The story narrates the original circumstances that led to the oracle (Gen 9:25ff; 12:2-3; 15:18; 27:28ff; etc.). These explanations were found to be so satisfactory that they gave rise to a specific literary type, the blessing (cf. comm. on Genesis 49). However childish they seem to us, however incapable these ancients were of arriving at a correct explanation of things, we must not fail to recognize the profundity that speaks out of these poetic stories. The contemporary relationships between peoples (this is what the narratives presuppose) were not due to chance, but had their causes in events that took place of old. They were in a certain sense predestined. The ethnological stories contain the beginnings of a philosophy of history.

Side by side with these are etymological motifs, which are the beginnings of the science of languages. Ancient Israel reflected much on the origin and proper meaning of the names of mountains, wells, sanctuaries, and cities. The names were not a matter of indifference to them as they are to us. They were convinced that names must stand in some sort of relationship to things. In many cases it was quite impossible for this ancient people to give a correct explanation. Names, in Israel as with other people, are the oldest material of language. They originate from extinct peoples or from an older stage of the language. Many German names like Rhein, Mosel, Neckar, Harz, Berlin, Ludwig, etc., are not obvious to one who has had no education in languages. Indeed, it is precisely because of their rarity that such words would have attracted the attention of ancient people. Ancient Israel explained these names naturally and without any scholarly wit on the basis of then current language. It associated an old name with a modern word which sounded more or less the same, and narrated a brief story to give the reason why that word was uttered only there and so had persisted as a name. We also have similar popular etymologies.

> "Ah Alm" (*Ach Allm*) groaned once a knight;
> the murderer struck him down;
> "Almighty" (*Allmächt'gen*) would he cry;
> thence comes the castle's name.
>
> —Ludwig Uhland, *Die Schlacht bei Reutlingen*

The *Langobards* were earlier known as *Winili*. Once during war the *Winili* women disguised themselves with beards. When Wodan looked through his window early in the morning and saw them, he said: "What sort of longbeards are they?" Since that time the *Winili* have called themselves "longbeards," i.e., *Langobards* (Grimm, *Deutsche Sagen*, No. 389). The Wartburg is said to derive its name from the story of a count who lost his way while hunting there. He said: "Wait (*wart'*), mountain (*Burg*), you must become a fortress for me!"

The same sorts of stories are found very often in Genesis, and later. The city Babel is so called because God "confused" (*bll*) languages there (Gen 11:9). "Jacob" is explained as "he takes by the heel," because at birth he grasped the heel of his twin brother, whom he grudged the right of firstborn (Gen 25:26). Zoar means "a little one," because Lot asked, "Let me escape there, is it not a little one?" (Gen 19:20, 22). Beer-sheba is the "well of seven," because Abraham presented Abimelech with seven lambs there (Gen 21:28ff). "Isaac" (*yiṣḥāq*) is thus called because his mother laughed (*ṣḥq*) when his birth was announced to her (Gen 18:12). And there are numerous other examples. Most of these explanations are extremely naive; one only has to think of the Hebrew story in which the Babylonian word Babel is explained from the Hebrew (*bll*). The Hebrews were often satisfied with like sounding approximations. Cain was said to be derived from *qānîtî*, "I have acquired" (Gen 4:1); Reuben from *rā'āh be'onyî*, "he has seen my distress" (Gen 29:32); and so on. Scholars have not always taken sufficient account of the naïveté of such etymologizing. Right up to recent times they have let themselves be led astray, thus often contributing to unsatisfactory explanations by use of modern methods. There is one case where many theologians are wont to describe one such explanation (very sophisticated to be sure) as an "authentic etymology" (Yahweh = "I am who I am," Exod 3:14); but etymologies are not revealed. Etymological stories, however, are particularly valuable for us because they are clear examples of the etiological type of story.

More important than these etymological stories are the cultic motifs whose purpose is to explain prescriptions for worship. Such prescriptions played a major role in the life of the ancients. There is a great number of customs of this sort which, already in the most ancient period accessible to us, were no longer comprehensible, either wholly or in part, to the one who carried them out. Customs are far more tenacious than attitudes, and cult is extraordinarily conservative. The situation is similar with us. Our worship underwent a mighty process of purification during the Reformation and again under rationalism; and now in many cases we do not understand (or we understand but partly) what we see and hear in our churches.

Ancient Israel reflected on the origin of many of its cultic customs. Even though the adults, dulled by constant usage, no longer took notice of the unusual and incomprehensible, they were roused from their torpor by the questions of the children. When children saw their fathers carrying out all sorts of unusual rites at the Feast of Passover, they asked—and this is expressly prescribed (cf. Exod 12:26; 13:14)—"What does this mean?" The story of the passover was then narrated to them. It was the same with the twelve stones at the Jordan (Josh 4:6). The father was to explain them to the children as a commemoration of the crossing of the river. These examples show us vividly how a story of this kind is an answer to a question.

The question is similarly raised about the origin of circumcision and of the sabbath — Why do we not eat the sinew of the hip (Gen 32:33)? For what reason does one anoint the holy stone at Bethel and offer the tithe there (Gen 28:18,22)? Why is it that we do not offer a child at Jeruel, the place where Isaac was offered (Gen 22:1-19), but a ram? [On Jeruel, see editor's note, p. 54.]

No Israelite could possibly have given the real reason for all these things; the reasons were far too old. But it was from this need that myth or story began. One narrated an event and thereby explained the holy custom — a long time ago something took place which naturally gave rise to what is now done; we carry out this custom in memory and imitation of what happened then. But the event which is meant to explain the present practice was said to have taken place regularly in the early period. Thus the ancient people presented the quite correct impression that the worship customs go back to time immemorial. The trees of Shechem (Gen 12:6) and Hebron (Gen 18:4) are older than Abraham! We practice circumcision because of Moses, whose firstborn was circumcised in place of him, and whose blood God wanted (Exod 4:14ff). We rest on the seventh day because God rested on the seventh day at the creation of the world (Gen 2:2-3; which is a myth, because it is God himself who is acting). The sinew of the hip is sacred to us because Jacob struck God or, as was said later, God struck Jacob there at Penuel (Gen 32:33; comm. p. 363). Jacob was the first to anoint the stone at Bethel because he used it as a pillow when the divinity appeared to him (Gen 28:18). At Jeruel God first demanded
▶ Abraham's child, but was then satisfied with the ram (Genesis 22).

On such occasions we hear continually of particular places, Bethel, Penuel, Shechem, Beer-sheba, Lahai-roi, Jeruel, etc., and of the trees, springs, and memorial stones there. These were the primal sanctuaries of the tribes and generations of Israel. A remote age had perceived immediately something of the very divinity itself in these elements of nature; but a later age, to which this link no longer appeared so patently obvious, raised the question: Why is it that this place and this symbol are so sacred? The stock answer was that it was because the divinity appeared to the ancestor there. We honor God there in memory of this elemental revelation. The cult story, then, had its origin (and this is of the utmost importance for the history of religion) in a time when the religious sense no longer had immediate experience of the sacredness of the place or natural object, and no longer understood the meaning of the sacred custom. The immediate impression of the sacredness of the holy symbol became in the story a unique experience of the primal ancestor, and the internal conviction was objectivized in an external event. The story then had to establish how God and the tribal ancestor happened to meet at this place. Abraham was sitting under a tree in the midday heat when the men appeared before him; hence the tree is holy (Gen 18:1ff). The well in the desert, Lahai-roi, became Ishmael's sanctuary because his mother met God there on her flight in the desert and he comforted her (Gen 16:7ff). Jacob happened to pass the night at a particular place, lay down with a stone under his head, and then saw a ladder reaching to heaven; hence the stone is our sanctuary (Gen 28:10ff). Moses happened to come to the holy mountain and thornbush with his herds (Exod 3:1ff). Each of the more important sanctuaries of Israel would have had a story of origin of this kind.

We can well imagine that such sanctuary stories were originally narrated on the occasion of the solemn festival at the particular place; Passover and the exodus story, Purim and the Esther legend, the Babylonian New Year feast and the creation hymn, all belong together. Our own Christmas and Easter would be quite unthinkable without their proper stories.

These cult stories are very useful to us because we learn from them of the sacred places and customs of Israel, and because they transplant us into the living world of ancient religious experience. They are our main sources for the oldest religion of Israel. Genesis is full of them, and there are a few in the later books. Almost everywhere that God appears at a particular place, there is a story of ◄ this sort at base. We have in them the beginnings of the history of religion.

In addition, there is a series of different kinds of story motifs, of which we will mention here only one, the geological. Its purpose is to explain the origin of a locality. Whence came the Dead Sea with its gruesome wasteland? The region was cursed by God because of the abominable sin of its inhabitants (Genesis 19). Whence comes the pillar of salt there that looks like a woman? It is a woman, Lot's wife, turned into salt because she took a furtive glance at the secret of the divinity (Gen 19:26). How is it that the patch of land around Zoar was excepted from the general devastation? Because Yahweh spared it as a place of refuge for Lot (Gen 19:17ff).

All these etiological motifs are far removed from the modern sciences to which they correspond. We look on them with the same indulgence as one looks back on one's childhood. Yet they have their value even in our scientific age because, as they presuppose and portray particular situations, they present us with all important material for our knowledge of the ancient world.

The Mingling of Motifs

There are almost always a number of different motifs united in the stories and mingled together in a variety of ways. The story of Hagar's flight (Genesis 16) is ethnographic inasmuch as it portrays Ishmael's way of life. It is ethnological inasmuch as it intends to explain this situation. A part of it is cultic, giving the reason why Lahai-roi is sacred. And it is also etymological because it explains the names Ishmael and Lahai-roi. The Bethel story (Gen 28:10ff) explains both the name and the cult there. The Beer-sheba stories (Gen 21:22ff; 26) contain historical fragments in that they tell of a treaty which peoples made there. At the same time they are cultic, explaining the sacredness of the place. Finally, they are also etymological. The Penuel story (Gen 32:23ff) explains the sacredness of the place, the names Penuel and Israel, and why the sinew of the hip is not eaten. And so on.

In the older narratives of Genesis the etymological motifs never appear independently, but are only subsidiary. Cases in which they prevail or even fill out the whole narrative are due to later narrative inventiveness. This is the case in the meeting of Jacob and Esau (comm. p. 356), and is particularly obvious in the account of the birth of the sons of Jacob (comm. p. 346). [B.D. Eerdmans's judgment in *Alttest. Studien* II, p. 49 that "the majority of stories" arose out of the names, is superficial. As has been shown above, the stories are due to quite different causes. In the oldest stories, those about Hebron, Sodom, Jacob and Laban, the etymological motif is well in the background.]

This shows how the stories grew in many cases. Hence it is very clear that, with the majority of etymological motifs, those parts of the stories which explain the names were created precisely for that purpose. Abraham's gift of seven lambs to Abimelech at Beer-sheba (Gen 21:28ff) was certainly invented to explain the name. The same holds for the laughter of Isaac's mother (Gen 18:12ff). What is told

about Judah's sons—Er, Onan, Shelah, Perez and Zerah (Genesis 38)—is in essence nothing other than the history of the families of Judah. Similarly, in the story of Shechem (Genesis 34) it is fairly certain that one can read the circumstances of an attack on Shechem. ◄
There are, however, a number of stories or parts of stories which do not contain motifs that are readily apparent to us. This would include large sections of the Joseph narrative (comm. p. 399). Likewise, the main motif of the Jacob-Laban story, a narrative of deceptions, is neither historical echo nor etiology. The same is true of Jacob's meeting with Rachel at the well, and a number of other stories. But even when the motifs in a story are explainable, we notice very often that the story as a whole is not to be explained by them, and that it contains pieces of greater or lesser length which lie outside any such explanation. The migrations of Abraham and Isaac to Gerar reflect something or other that is historical, but the surrender and recovery of the wife must have had a different origin (comm. p. 173). The attack on Shechem is historical, but what happened to Dinah is not (comm. p. 371). In the story of Tamar one must distinguish between the tribal element and the obscure material that deals with Tamar's required marriage (comm. p. 419). The Cain story reflects ethnographic material in that it portrays the current situation of Cain. But that he had a brother Abel whom he murdered is not to be so explained (comm. p. 48). It is worthy of special note that the element that we cannot explain is in each case the kernel of the story.

In many cases we learn from parallels which present history as story (see chapter 5) that the story contains material that has come from elsewhere (e.g., the Hebron story, the story of Sodom, of Lot's daughters, of the sacrifice of Isaac, of Jacob and Rachel at the well, of Jacob's struggle at Penuel, and in particular of the adulterous Egyptian wife, etc.). It is quite obvious in the stories of Jacob and Esau (comm. pp. 295-296, 315-316), and of the treaty of Jacob with Laban (comm. p. 352), that subsequent Israelite interest has taken over the story and that dimensions of Israelite history have entered into it. Jacob and Esau have been equated with the peoples Israel and Edom, and the treaty between Jacob and Laban has been given an ethnohistorical meaning. But we can also imagine the opposite case where a story arose out of a historical event or in order to answer a question, and has been heavily elaborated by the addition of all sorts of poetic and other motifs. This could be the case, for example, with the stories of Dinah and Tamar. Drawing together all these observations which hold more or less true for every ancient story, we come to the conclusion that *the material treated in the patriarchal stories is on the whole neither historical nor etiological in origin.* Many of the narratives or their raw material must have already existed before they acquired their new meaning in the life of Israel. [Cf. E. Meyer, *Israeliten* (1906) 250-251, who has helped me here; also W. Wundt, *Völkerpsychologie* II, 3 (1909):360, 418; and H. Gressmann, *ZAW* 30 (1910):11ff, 18, 20, 23, who have also reached this conclusion.] They must have circulated for a long time as pleasant stories, and in origin were pure products of the creative spirit. Such passages, which do not admit of an explanation, are, for want of a better word, called "story-like" (*novellistisch*) in the commentary; perhaps "fable-like" (*märchenhaft*) would be a better term. [Translator—or "fabulous" in the original and literal meaning of the word. Footnote—see chapter 3; H. Gressmann, *ZAW* 30 (1910):12ff, calls these primal narratives "(folk) tales" (*Märchen*). However, it should be noted that in Genesis the fantastic (which is characteristic of the folk tale) is generally absent, and that, in contrast to folk tales, the narratives are very tautly put together.]

3
THE ARTISTIC FORM
OF THE STORIES IN GENESIS

Rhythm and Style in Biblical Story

The beauty of the stories in Genesis has always been a delight to sensitive readers, and it is not by chance that painters have so readily taken material from this book for their pictures. Scholars, however, have been less frequently moved by this beauty, often because the esthetic sense seemed to them incompatible with serious scholarship. We certainly do not share this prejudice, and are of the opinion that whoever passes over these stories without attention to their artistic form is not only deprived of a great pleasure, but is also unable to carry out properly the scholarly duty of understanding Genesis. Indeed, scholarship is fully justified in asking the question, Of what does the specific beauty of these stories consist? The answer penetrates deeply into their content and religion.

The first question is, Are these narratives prose or poetry? Hitherto the general opinion has been that all narratives in the Old Testament are prose. But this has been contested by the German philologist Ed. Sievers whose work on Hebrew meter is seminal. In a grand work, admirable in many respects, Sievers produced a metrically divided Genesis (*Metrische Studien II, Hebräische Genesis,* 1904, 1905).

What is the style of Genesis like? It is characteristic of the narratives of Genesis, as of all narratives in the Old Testament, that it displays no elevated, animated style, but eschews any decorative speech. The narrator takes care to describe things clearly and in the simplest terms. There is no place here for an image, an oratorical expression, a decorative aside, a poetic link, or a detailed portrayal. Anything involving the emotions is well in the background in the narrative proper and dares take but a timid step forward in the oral

27

exchanges (an example of poetic expression is the speech in Gen 19:8). It is strange that the hot-blooded Hebrews narrate so calmly. These narrators seem to be a very different class of people from the burning prophets! And the characteristic division of thought into two sentences, what is called "parallelism of parts," so typical of Hebrew poetic style, is missing. It is this calmness and starkness of the narrative style that to a large extent constitutes the captivating, unadorned beauty of the ancient narratives. The "blessings of Jacob" (Genesis 49) are obvious exceptions to this, but they are not narrative. Rather, they constitute a poem, and so do not really belong to Genesis. In certain places, when the narrative moves to a climax, particularly when the story reports words which bring about something marvelous, the language rises to animated, poetic style. This occurs also in fairy tales where the magic words are usually in poetic form. It is also the case in the older Brahman and Buddhist literature: "Strophes, which bring together the most important elements, statements and the moral of the narrative in the poetic form of maxims," interrupt the epic prose. [Cf. Geldner, "Gāthā," *RGG*.] It is similar with modern tribal stories translated from Tigre by E. Littmann [*Orient. Studien*, Th. Noldeke issue, pp. 947, 953ff], with the nordic court poets and singers and the Irish poets.

Unless we are mistaken, these remarks on style are decisive in judging the rhythmic form of the narratives. *Such straightforward narratives cannot follow a strict rhythmic scansion.* We find no trace of any fixed rhythm which determines the choice or position of the words and to which, for better or worse, they must conform. There are no patch-words which are unnecessary for meaning but are there only to complete the metric pattern. There are no deviations, great or small, from ordinary speech, due to the demands of rhythm, such as occur throughout the rhyming chronicles of the Middle Ages, and to which Sievers incorrectly appeals (I, 376). What gives the deceptive impression of meter is nothing other than the anapaestic rhythm of the Hebrew words and the practice of the language of joining two or three emphatic words in close logical proximity to each other. Certainly, good Hebrew prose has a fine rhythmic euphony which can be defined more precisely. However, these prose rhythms are not to be equated with regular "even" meters, but only with the loosest "compound meters" of poetry (Sievers I, 129ff). [Note: the translator has omitted here a long footnote of one and a half pages in

which Gunkel demonstrates under five headings how, in his opinion,
Sievers's attempt to put Genesis into meter has foundered.]

Story in Oral Tradition

As the stories were already very old when they were written
down (see chapter 4), it is natural that the language of Genesis is
archaic; and this should come through in translation. We know of ◄
biblical and extrabiblical variants of individual stories (particularly of
the creation, flood and paradise stories) — variants which have a rigid
rhythmic form and an animated, poetic style. Because these variants
are older than those in Genesis, one may perhaps surmise that some
of the latter once possessed some poetic form. The older type of
poetic style would have differed from the later type of prose style
much as the German heroic song does from the later "popular prose
romance." However, the surmise of such an older poetic form would
be valid only for myths and perhaps the sanctuary stories (see below).
A second question is, Were these imaginative works handed
down in popular tradition or were they the products of individual
poets? Modern scholars have in principle correctly decided that
Genesis is the setting down in writing of popular tradition, and we are
now in a position to clarify how such "popular traditions" arose.
Naturally each was at base the work of an individual. Now it is
common to such popular traditions that we do not observe them in
the process of formation, just as we do not observe language in
process. When we first hear of them, they always appear as ancient
material inherited from our forefathers. There was a long interval
between the poet who first gave them shape and the time when they
were passed on to us. During this interval the story was narrated
over and over from generation to generation and passed through
many hands. However faithfully the stories were transmitted, they
were nevertheless reshaped on their path through the centuries (see
chapter 4). Thus the story is ultimately a creation of the people in
common.
Reshaping of the story took place unconsciously, at least in the
earlier stages. One can only speak of conscious recasting in its latest
formations. *Narrator and hearer both regarded the stories as true
accounts.* Our historical books show that this was true of the stories
of the Old Testament as well. The biblical narrators pass almost
imperceptibly from stories to properly historical narratives and go on

to mingle the fabulous with the historical. This follows also from the very nature of stories, which seriously aimed to substantiate contemporary realities—because the woman was taken from the rib of the man, man longs for her company. For the narrator this account was not the clothing of an idea in poetic dress, but an event that really took place. This is entirely natural since story stems from times and circles which did not yet have the intellectual ability to distinguish clearly between poetic imagination and reality. Modern scholars have fallen into no small error by maintaining that the paradise story is an allegory that had no intention of being reality.

Moreover, precisely because the story was created by the whole people, it is also the expression of their spirit. This is of the utmost importance for our utilization of the testimony of Genesis. We are justified in holding that the judgments and views which Genesis lays before us are the common property of a wider circle.

We must therefore look at Genesis first in the form in which it existed in oral tradition, and if we want to understand the stories we must picture the situation in which they would have been narrated. We hear of such situations in Exod 12:26-27; 13:11-12; and Josh 4:6. When children asked about the reason for a sacred custom or the meaning of a sacred symbol, their fathers answered them by narrating a story. One can imagine, then, how the story of Sodom was narrated looking out over the Dead Sea, and the Bethel story on the heights of Bethel. But the usual situation that we must bear in mind is this: on the long winter evenings the family would sit around the fireside. The adults, and especially the children, listened attentively to fine old stories from distant times—stories often heard and always in demand. We approach and listen with them. Many of the stories, as we shall see below, have such a well formed, artistic style that in this form they can scarcely be considered popular creations. Rather, we must assume that there was a position of popular storyteller in Israel and among the Arabs, as among many peoples past and present. These storytellers were skilled in story and song, moved around the land, and could be found at popular festivals.

We have seen above that the present prose form of at least some of the stories was perhaps preceded by a poetic form. We can consider these songs as having been set in another context. Following the pattern of the Babylonian poem of creation, which in form is a New Year's hymn to Marduk, we can perhaps imagine that the cult stories go back to sanctuary hymns which were sung by the priests on solemn feasts at the holy place (see below). However this may be, the received stories were certainly no longer sung, nor do they belong in their present form to the holy places themselves, as their colorless character shows. They belong to popular tradition.

Units in Story

A new question (and again a basic one) is, Which unit is the determinative one for Genesis research — the one that we ought primarily to study and have the benefit of? A series of different units | would come into consideration here. The most extensive is the whole Pentateuch, then Genesis, then the book of individual stories that preceded it, then the individual stories which make up the book. Among these one must distinguish the independent individual stories, such as the narratives of Hagar's flight (Genesis 16), the sacrifice of Isaac (Genesis 22), and certain cycles of stories, such as those dealing with the fortunes of Abraham and Lot up to the birth of their sons, or those which bring Jacob's experiences with Esau and Laban together into a single narrative, or those in which Joseph is the hero. We must consider all these units. But the first question is, Which of these is to be given retrospective priority; i.e., which of these different units is the original one in oral tradition?

The same question recurs in many similar cases: What is the authoritative unit, the book of song, the individual collection within it, or the individual song? Is it the gospel, the discourse, or the individual saying of Jesus that has been passed on? Is it the whole Apocalypse, or the individual apocalyptic texts or the individual vision? It is of decisive importance for the understanding of Genesis that one faces this question squarely and answers it correctly. *Popular story of its very nature takes the form of the individual story.* ◄ Only later do collectors bring a number of these together, or poets fashion larger artistic patterns out of them. This was also the case with the popular stories of the Hebrews, as is clearly evident from the stories of Genesis in their present form. Each individual story which is preserved in its old form is a whole in itself. It has a clear beginning and a readily recognizable end.

Let us compare some examples. Abraham wanted to acquire a wife for his son. As he was too old himself, he sent his oldest servant. This is the beginning of the narrative (Genesis 24). Then comes the account of how the servant found the right girl and brought her home. The old master had died in the meantime, so the young man received the bride and "was comforted after his father's death." The story ends here. In another story Abraham was instructed by God to sacrifice his son. This is the *exposé*. It is an entirely new beginning (Genesis 22). Then comes the account of how Abraham carried out his resolve and almost completed it, but at the last moment God himself forestalled the sacrifice. Isaac was preserved for Abraham. "Then they went back together to Beer-sheba." On each occasion the narrative begins in such a way that one is aware that something new is starting here. Likewise, the narrative concludes clearly with the plot successfully settled, so that no one can say, Where to from here? The unity of the individual story is likewise manifest from the unified mood that sustains it. Emotion dominates in the story of the sacrifice of Isaac (Genesis 22), humor in Jacob's deception of Isaac (Genesis 27), moral seriousness in the story of Sodom (Genesis 19), awe before the all powerful God in the narrative of the tower (Genesis 11). Many narratives would be completely destroyed if another followed immediately so as to wrench the reader violently from one mood to another. Rather, every judicious narrator pauses after completing a story in order to give the imagination time to recuperate, to allow the listeners to reflect on what they have heard, and to let the mood resonate. For example, whoever has participated in the story of the sacrifice of Isaac needs to rest and recover from the violent emotion of the experience. Those narratives in particular which aim at giving the reason for a current situation (see chapter 2) require a pause at the end so that the listeners can compare the prophetic word pronounced in the narrative with the current fulfillment. One may recall, for example, the conclusions of the paradise story, of the flood narrative, and of Noah's drunkenness.

Later on, larger units or cycles of stories were formed in which individual stories were more or less artificially put together. But even in these cases there is usually no difficulty in separating out the original individual pieces from the transition passages. The cycle of stories about Abraham and Lot, for instance, breaks down as follows:

1) Abraham and Lot's immigration into Canaan
2) Their parting at Bethel
3) The appearance of God at Hebron
4) The destruction of Sodom
5) The birth of Ammon and Moab
6) The birth of Isaac

The Jacob-Esau-Laban cycle consists of the stories about Jacob and Esau, Jacob and Laban, the origin of the twelve tribes, and some additional individual cult stories. In the Joseph story, too, the narratives of Joseph's experiences with his brothers, of Potiphar's wife, of the explanation of the dreams in prison, of the Pharaoh's dreams, of the agricultural arrangements in Egypt (Gen 47:13ff), are in marked contrast to each other.

The conclusion is thus inescapable that each individual story must always be first explained of itself. *The more independent a narrative, the more certainly it is preserved in its old form.* However, the link which exists between the individual stories is in many cases of later origin—if not a simple insertion of the expositor. ["The individuality of the single narrative is what is essential and original; the context is secondary and has only been introduced with the collection and the fixing in writing," J. Wellhausen, *Prolegomena,* 6th ed., p. 334.] As an example of an ancient story which presupposes virtually nothing, one could offer the narrative of Hagar's flight (Genesis 16). All we need to know is that there is a man named Abraham and a woman named Sarah; the story says everything else. An example of a later narrative is the story of the wooing of Rebekah (Genesis 24). This story presupposes a whole series of details which have their setting in other accounts—Abraham's family relationship and departure, the promise made at the departure, the fact that Isaac was the son of his old age and his only son, and so on. It is the individual story, therefore, to which we have to give primary consideration.

The Length and the Arrangement of the Story

What is the span of such a narrative? Many of the narratives in Genesis scarcely extend beyond ten verses; e.g., Noah's drunkenness, the tower, Abraham's journey down to Egypt, Hagar's flight (Genesis 16), Ishmael's expulsion (Gen 21:8ff), Abraham's trial (Genesis 22), Jacob at Bethel (Gen 28:10ff) and at Penuel (Gen 32:25ff). Besides these very short stories there is a number of "detailed" narratives which cover as much as a chapter, such as the paradise story, the narratives of Cain's murder of his brother, the flood, the appearance of the divinity at Hebron (Genesis 18), Rebekah's betrothal (Genesis 24), and Jacob's deception of Isaac (Genesis 27). Only the cycles of stories (which are later) exceed these in size.

The length of the stories differs considerably from that of our present-day creations. Even the most intricate arrangements in Genesis, such as the Joseph story, are very modest in extent when judged by current standards. But the older stories are extraordinarily short according to modern tastes, and this is one of their unique characteristics. They deal with very simple events which can be portrayed adequately in a few words. Such a span accords alike with the art of the storyteller and the listener's capacity for comprehension. The first storytellers were not capable of fashioning extensive works of art. Nor could they have expected their listeners to follow them all week or even all day with undiminished attention. Rather, antiquity was satisfied with very short works which scarcely occupied a quarter of an hour. When the story was over, the listener's imagination had had enough and his capacity for comprehension was exhausted. At most, we can suppose that afterwards the listeners wanted to hear the story again, just as do our children.

On the other hand, the biblical narratives do demonstrate that a later age was no longer content with the very short original stories. An esthetic sense, grown to maturity, required more space in which to express itself. The result was longer creations. This growth in the stories was encouraged by the fact that they were being put into writing—what is written is of its nature more prolix than what is spoken. The eye can take in larger units as it reads than can the ear as it hears. Thence follows a criterion for the age of the stories which, of course, must be used with caution: *the briefer a story, the more likely it is to have been preserved in its old form.*

Such brevity is, as we have seen, indicative of the poverty of this ancient art. At the same time, however, this poverty had certain advantages. The narrow span within which the storyteller had to move made it necessary to focus all of his or her artistic power onto one tiny spot. However brief and condensed these works may be, their effect is powerful. Hence the limited power of comprehension of which these short works of art are witness, led to the narratives being given a form which is as clear and carefully arranged as is possible.

In order to grasp this, one should observe the arrangement of the narrative above all else. The narratives (not only those that are lengthier, but also the briefest ones) are divided with extraordinary sharpness into different scenes. By "scenes" we mean those smaller parts of a narrative which are distinguished by a change of person, place, or action. For example, the story of Noah's drunkenness (Gen 9:20ff) is arranged as follows:

Exposé: Noah's drunkenness
I. The events:
   1. Canaan's shamelessness
   2. The piety of Shem and Japheth
II. The pronouncements:
   1. on Canaan
   2. on Japheth and Shem

The paradise story (Genesis 3) is arranged in this manner:
I. The sin:
   1. The snake tempts the woman
   2. The woman and the man sin
   3. The consequences: loss of innocence
II. The trial
III. The punishment:
   1. The curse on the snake
   2. The curse on the woman
   3. The curse on the man
IV. Conclusion: the expulsion

Such nice, clear divisions confer on the narratives the stamp of clarity, a precondition for any esthetic effect. The whole falls into divisions and subdivisions which themselves are arranged in a very orderly manner and whose relationship to each other is quite clear. These arrangements are not the result of applied ingenuity, but proceed naturally from the thing itself. For example, in the paradise story the arrangement corresponds admirably to the content. The sin follows the sequence: snake, woman, man; the trial follows the reverse sequence: man, woman, snake; the punishment strikes the chief offender first, and so the original sequence appears again: snake, woman, man. Hence the modern reader is advised to pay attention to the arrangement because he or she then has access to the progress of the action.

The Number of Characters in the Story

Furthermore, the ancient storyteller did not require the listeners to fix their attention simultaneously on several characters, as does the present-day novelist. Rather, only a very few appear at a time.

The minimum, of course, is two, because at least two are necessary for the narrative to develop. There are two persons in the narrative of the separation of Abraham and Lot (Genesis 13), of Esau's sale of his birthright (Gen 25:29ff), and in the story of Penuel (Gen 32:23ff). There are three characters in the story of the creation of the woman (God, the man, the woman), in the story of Cain's fratricide (God, Cain, Abel), in the story of Lot in the cave (Gen 19:30ff), and in that of the sacrifice of Isaac (Genesis 22). There are four in the paradise story, in Abraham's journey down to Egypt (Gen 12:10ff), in Hagar's flight (Genesis 16), and in Jacob's deception of Isaac (Genesis 27). Nevertheless, there are some narratives in which several persons appear, as in the detailed account of the wooing of Rebekah, and particularly in the narratives of the sons of Jacob. But here, too, the storyteller was concerned for simplicity and good arrangement. In many cases where several characters appear, they are treated as a unit; they think and want alike and act in unison. In the narratives of the flood and the tower, humankind acts as one person. So do the brothers Shem and Japheth (Gen 9:23), the three men at Hebron and Sodom (according to the original form of the narrative, Genesis 18-19), Lot's son-in-law at Sodom (Gen 19:14), Pharaoh's courtiers (Gen 12:15), the citizens of Shechem, the brothers of Dinah (Genesis 34), the citizens of Timnah (Gen 38:21), etc.

This accords with the situation in those ancient times when the individual was separated from the larger community far less than today. At the same time, the narrators grouped together different persons because of their inability to perceive and present differences between individuals. The Joseph story is a very clear example of how little even an esthetically developed narrator was capable of characterizing individuals. The narrative set Joseph and the eleven over against each other. It does single out Joseph's full brother, the youngest, Benjamin. Reuben (Judah) also had a special place among the ten. But this exhausted the narrator's power to draw characters. He or she could not comprehend the other nine as individuals. They were simply "the brothers."

Further simplicity was achieved by the arrangement which, as we have seen, broke the narrative into clearly defined scenes. It is rare that all persons in the narrative appear at the same time; there are almost always just a few, often only two. [One of A. Olrik's "epic laws of folk narrative" is that two is the highest number of persons who appear at the same time: "only two persons ever appear on the stage at the same time." This is generally also the case in Genesis. *Zeit. für deutsches Altertum*, 51 (1909) 1-12; Eng. "Epic Laws of Folk Narrative," in Alan Dundes, ed., *The Study of Folklore*, New Jersey: Prentice-Hall, 1965, pp. 129-141.] One may compare the scenes in the story of the suit for Rebekah (Genesis 24). The first scene shows Abraham and the servant; the second, the servant alone on his journey and at the well; the third, the servant and the girl; the fourth, the girl and her family; the fifth (the principal scene), the servant with the girl and her family; the sixth, the servant on his return journey with the girl; the last, these two and Isaac. In the story of Ishmael's expulsion (Gen 21:4ff) we see successively: Sarah as she hears Ishmael laughing and as she takes up the matter with Abraham, Abraham as he expels Hagar, Hagar alone with the child in the desert, and finally the rescue by the angel. The story of Jacob's trickery (Genesis 27) deals first with Isaac and Esau, then with Rebekah and Jacob, next with Jacob and Isaac, then with Esau and Isaac, then with Esau's hate for Jacob, and finally with Rebekah's advice to Jacob. It was the particular task of the narrator to justify this succession of scenes. However, there was no reluctance to occasionally simply allow a character to drop out, as with the snake after the temptation (Gen 3:5), or Rebekah after Jacob's flight from Esau (i.e., following Genesis 27).

Thanks to this arrangement the narrative gains greatly in clarity. The listener is not forced to face a bewildering number of people at the same time, but can look at them one after the other. There is time to consider them quietly and impress them on the memory. Only at the high points of the action are all the characters there together, as in the final scene of a modern drama; for example, the paradise story (Gen 3:14ff), Noah's drunkenness (Gen 9:24ff), and the conclusion of the Joseph story (Gen 46:29ff). But even there the narrators deem some division necessary. They would not have been capable of portraying a conversation between several persons. So at the end of the paradise story God did not reproach all the guilty parties with their sins in one common address, but turned first to the snake, then to the woman, and finally to the man. Elsewhere as well, the style consists of breaking down the speeches into a series of dialogues.

Principal and Secondary Characters

Moreover, the general view of the different characters is brought
out by the frequent distinction between principal and secondary
characters. The listener does not have to look far to find which
character is to claim attention; the narrator makes this very clear by
the simple fact that the most important character is the one most
often mentioned. Hence, the patriarchs themselves are the main
characters in most of the patriarchal narratives.

In the following, the characters in each narrative are arranged in
their order of importance to the narrator: Cain, Abel; Abraham,
Sarah, Pharaoh (Gen 12:10ff); Abraham, Lot (Gen 13:7ff); Hagar,
Sarah, Abraham (Genesis 16). The main characters in Genesis 24
are the servant and Rebekah. In Genesis 27, Jacob and Esau (the
parents being secondary characters); in the Jacob-Laban story, Jacob
and Laban are the main characters; the women are secondary.

One should not confuse sympathy and respect with interest.
Cain is more important to the artistic interest of the narrator than
Abel, and Hagar more than Sarah; the servant is the main character
in Genesis 24, while Abraham plays only a secondary role. In many
cases there is but a single character whose destiny we follow, notably
in the Joseph stories. ["There is always one formal main character,"
A. Olrik, p. 10; Eng. p. 139.]

Characterization

How are the characters that appear portrayed? What first
strikes us is the brevity with which the secondary characters are
treated. We are used to modern writers who, as far as possible,
present each character as a complete individual, even though with
only a few strokes. The method of the ancient storyteller was entirely
different. Secondary characters, be they permanent or occasional,
were drawn either sketchily or not at all. It is to be expected because
of ancient sentiment on the matter that the narrator did not feel
obliged to dwell on servants. Esau's (Gen 32:7) or Laban's (Gen
31:23ff) entourage are merely there in order to set forth the power of
these two. Similarly, the narrators did not think it necessary to give
details of the offenses of Pharaoh's chamberlains (Gen 40:1), to
describe Dinah's feelings (Genesis 34) or the feelings of Sarah on the
way down to Egypt (Gen 12:10ff). There is no characterization of

Judah's friend Hirah (Genesis 38). Er's offense is not mentioned.
Nothing of any significance is reported of Judah's wife nor of
Joseph's majordomos (Gen 43:16ff). And so on.   ◄
But even the description of the main characters is remarkably
meager by our standards. Very few qualities were attributed to
them—sometimes only one. Cain was envious of his brother.
Canaan was without shame, Shem and Japheth were chaste (Gen
9:20ff). In the story of the separation of Lot and Abraham (Gen
13:2ff), Lot was avaricious, Abraham accommodating. Abraham was
hospitable in the Hebron story (Genesis 18) and obedient to God's
command when he emigrated (Genesis 12). Jacob was strong and
courageous at Penuel (Gen 32:25ff), clever in his dealings with Esau,
and loving towards Rachel's sons in the Joseph story. The snake was
clever and malicious in the rather complicated story of the first sin,
the man and the woman were as inexperienced as children, the
woman was sweet-toothed and talkative, the man followed his wife.
Likewise, each of the individual stories knows only one of God's
attributes. He is for the most part the merciful helper, but in some
stories (e.g., the garden and the tower) he is the exalted Lord who
keeps the human race within limits.
The parsimony of story is striking. In modern works of creative
literature we are accustomed to encountering characters portrayed
with a complexity of qualities. But the art of the ancient narrators
was very different. It was, of course, conditioned by the circumstances of antiquity inasmuch as people of that time were simpler
than the complicated person of our own day. However, it would be a
mistake to think that these people were as simple as portrayed in the
stories. One only has to compare the character portrayals of the
more mature art of the two books of Samuel.
One learns from this example that there is more here than the
sort of abridgment of reality which is inherent in any artistic
presentation. What is given expression in Genesis is a particular
popular view of the human race—a limited view which was incapable
of comprehending and expressing the many sides of humanity, let
alone its totality. Story strove all the more, therefore, to grasp the
essential make-up of the person, and so shaped general types.
Hagar, then, was the servant maid who was favored (Genesis 16),
Sarah the jealous wife, Abraham the upright and patient husband. |
Rachel and Leah were types of "the loved one" and "the despised
one" (Gen 29:31ff). In the narrative of Abraham's journey into Egypt

(Gen 12:10ff) or in the Joseph story, Pharaoh acted precisely as the narrator expected that an oriental king would act; and the courtiers were simply courtiers. Abraham's servant was an old and faithful servant (Genesis 24); Isaac was a blind old man and Rebekah a scheming, cunning mother (Genesis 27). Abraham was the pious, obedient man as he emigrated and went to sacrifice Isaac (Genesis 22). A series of figures are types of peoples or of classes of people: the angry Cain, the shameless Canaan, the generous but thoughtless Esau, the cunning Laban, and the much cleverer Jacob (see chapter 2).

Again, it is undoubtedly a mark of an impoverished power of comprehension that the stories present us not so much with individual persons as with types. But the narrators knew well how to make a virtue out of necessity. Within the limits given them, their achievement was extraordinary. They grasped the types that they were able to observe with the same kind of clarity and sureness that enabled Egyptian artists to paint ethnic types. For this very reason many of the old stories still captivate the modern reader, even the uneducated. The stories very often portray that which is common to the human race, including situations that are immediately comprehensible even today. All the greater then is the pleasure they give to the specialist, offering in a very attractive form the most intimate insights into the workings and emotions of ancient people.

Story usually achieves such perspicacity by setting two main actors in opposition to each other: Jacob the clever shepherd and Esau the stupid hunter, the shameless Canaan and the chaste Shem and Japheth, the generous Joseph and his envious brothers, Abel the shepherd favored by God and Cain the hapless farmer, the ugly Leah and the beautiful Rachel, Lot with his open house, and the Sodomites who shamelessly abused the law of hospitality. [This is Olrik's "law of contrast," A. Olrik p. 6; Eng. p. 135.]

Incidentally, this simplicity of the characters also makes it obvious that the art of popular stories was far from being able to present any kind of character development. Everything of this sort that modern expositors think they have found in Genesis has been read into it. Jacob's "ambiguity" did not change. Joseph's brothers did not "improve" in the course of the narrative, but were merely punished.

While the individual stories essentially portray only one characteristic of the actors, the cycles of stories are in a position to give more detailed descriptions (though in their own peculiar way). Of course, the most prominent example of this is the picture of Joseph in the Joseph cycle. Each individual story portrays one or two aspects of his character. One story tells that he was loved by his father (and for this reason hated by his brothers) and that he had dreams foretelling the future (Genesis 39). A second reveals that everything prospered under his hand and that he was handsome and pure (Genesis 39). A third shows that he was able to interpret dreams (Genesis 40). A fourth points out his cleverness (Genesis 41), and so on. Only the synthesis of all these yields a complete picture.

The writers were remarkably reserved in the external descriptions of people. They let us know nothing about the hair, the color of the skin, the eyes or the clothing. Everywhere the normal Hebrew type was presupposed. Whenever there is a deviation from this rule, it is always for very definite reasons. Esau was red and hairy (Gen 25:25), obviously an anticipation of the people one associates with him; Joseph wore the sleeved tunic as a sign of his father's love (Genesis 37); Leah had weak eyes because Jacob rejected her (Gen 29:17).

If we ask what basic principle the narrators followed when at times they emphasized certain characteristics of their actors, it becomes clear that character was for the most part fully subordinate to action. That characteristic of the actors was portrayed which was necessary for the progress of the action. Everything else, whatever it may have been, was omitted. The story of Jacob's trickery (Genesis 27) relates how he, on his mother's advice, brought it about that his father Isaac blessed him, and not Esau. Jacob is the clever one; he deceived. Esau was stupid; he let himself be disadvantaged. Isaac was blind and thus easily deceived. Rebekah was cunning; she gave shrewd advice and sided with Jacob. In a more detailed narrative, this was joined with other qualities. Jacob was a shepherd and stayed at home with his mother. Esau was a hunter, and his father liked the game he brought in. The modern writer would add a number of further qualities so as to present a colorful and lively picture. The ancient narrators despised this. Their esthetic interest is clear; it was the action that mattered above all else—the drawing of characters was secondary.

Character Development

How did the storytellers present the character of their heroes?
The modern creative writer is wont to spend a long time in tracing
the development of his characters' thoughts and moods. So one is
astounded on coming to Genesis to find how little is said about the
inner being of its heroes. Very rarely does Genesis come to terms
with the thoughts of the actors — the woman as she looked longingly
at the tree in the garden (Gen 3:6), Noah when he sent out the birds
"to see if the water had abated from the earth" (Gen 8:8), Lot's
sons-in-law when they thought that their father-in-law was joking
(Gen 19:14), Isaac when he was afraid that the men of Gerar would
kill him because of his wife (Gen 26:7), Jacob when he cleverly
planned to avert the vengeance of his brother Esau (Gen 32:9, 21),
and so on. But such comments are not the rule in the stories of
Genesis. The storyteller was for the most part satisfied with very
brief remarks, such as "he became angry" (Gen 4:5; 30:2; 31:36; 34:7;
39:19; 40:2), "he was afraid (Gen 26:7; 28:17; 32:8), "he was
comforted" (Gen 24:67), "he loved her" (Gen 24:67; 29:18; 34:3;
37:3), "she became jealous" (Gen 30:1), "he was put out" (Gen 27:33),
"they hated him" (Gen 37:4), and so on.

Most often, however, we find not the slightest word about the
thoughts and feelings of the actors concerned. This omission is
sometimes quite surprising to us. The storyteller was silent, for
example, about the reasons why God forbade humans access to the
tree in the garden (Gen 2:17). Nothing is said of the reasons why the
snake wanted to seduce the first couple. There is not a word about
Abraham's feelings as he left his homeland (Genesis 12), nor of
Noah's as he entered the ark (Gen 7:7). We hear nothing of Noah's
anger at Canaan's shamelessness (Gen 9:24), of Jacob's disap-
pointment when Laban deceived him with Leah (Gen 29:35), or of
Hagar's joy when the promise was communicated to her that Ishmael
was to become a people (Gen 21:18). There is not even a word
about a mother's joy when she held her first son in her arms (Gen
4:1; 21:6; 25:24ff). The story of the sacrifice of Isaac (Genesis 22) is
the most striking example. What present-day writer would fail to
describe Abraham's internal turmoil as his obedience in faith won the
difficult struggle over his fatherly love, and as his grief was finally
turned to joy?

What is the reason for this peculiar phenomenon? An example like Gen 19:27-28 can teach us. As Abraham gazed over Sodom, he heard the portentous utterance of the three men. They wanted, so they said, to go down to Sodom to enquire about the guilt of the city (Gen 18:20-21). These words kept running through his mind. The next morning he rose and went to the same place. He wanted to see if anything had happened to Sodom during the night. Indeed, he saw that something or other had happened under the smoke, but the smoke blotted out the region. What was actually going on, he could not make out. For the narrator, the value of this short scene did not lie in what really happened, but in the thoughts that Abraham must have had. Nevertheless they were not described. We are given only the external circumstances and must supply the main material ourselves. The narrator had an eye for the hero's internal state, but was unable to comprehend it with sufficient clarity to be able to adequately express it in words.

This is typical of Genesis. There are many occasions where the modern writer would describe a psychological confrontation, but in which the ancient storyteller preferred an action. [".... each attribute of a person or thing must be expressed in actions — otherwise it is nothing," A. Olrik, p. 8; Eng. p. 137.] There is, for example, no contrast between the interior state of the couple before and after the fall — a single meaningful example describes all (Gen 2:25; 3:7). The storyteller said nothing of Adam's thoughts when the woman offered him the forbidden fruit, simply that he ate. He or she did not lay bare the feelings of the hospitable Abraham, but narrated how he received the three men (Gen 18:2ff). There is no word about Shem and Japheth feeling chaste and respectful, only that they acted that way (Gen 9:23). It is not said that Joseph was touched when he saw Benjamin again, but that he turned aside to weep (Gen 42:24; 43:30). Nor was it related that Hagar felt her maternal pride hurt when she was mistreated by Sarah, only that she ran away from her mistress (Gen 16:6). It was not stated that Laban was blinded by the stranger's gold, simply that he hastened to invite him (Gen 24:30-31); nor that Abraham's obedience to God triumphed over his father's love, but only that he rose up at once (Gen 22:3). Likewise, it was not stated that Tamar remained loyal to her husband in his grave, only that she prepared to raise children from his seed (Genesis 38).

One sees, then, where the storytellers put their main emphasis.
They had not the attitude of modern writers who regard the inner
| being of a human as the most interesting and most deserving object
of their art. Rather, their taste was childlike and they preferred to
dwell on events that affect the external senses. It is here that they
really achieved something. They understood very well how to select
just that action which is most significant for the hero's spiritual state.
| How could respect and modesty be presented better than in the story
of Shem and Japheth? How could a mother's love be better shown
than in the story of Hagar? – she gave her son a drink (Gen 21:19), it
is not said that she herself drank. How could hospitality be better
described than by Abraham's response at Hebron (Gen 18:2ff)?
Note also the insight and simplicity with which the innocence and
awareness of the first couple was illustrated by nakedness and
clothing (Gen 2:25; 3:7). These accomplished artists may not have
been versed in reflective discourse, but they were masters of the
visual. It is this marvelous art of indirect portrayal of people by
means of actions that above all makes the stories so vivid. ["The
story invariably rises to peaks in the form of one or more major
tableaux scenes," A. Olrik, p. 9; Eng. p. 138.] However little the most
ancient storytellers were able to speak of the inner being, one
nevertheless has the impression that they have offered us a glimpse
into the innermost heart of their heroes. These figures live before
our eyes, and so the modern reader, charmed by the transparent
clarity of these old stories, can completely forget what they lack.

But even when the narrator says nothing of the inner being of
the heroes, all was not entirely lost on the listener. We must
remember at this point that we have before us stories which were
narrated orally. Between narrator and listener there is a bond
beyond that of words. There is the tone of voice, the expression of
face, or some movement of the hand. Joy and pain, love, anger, envy,
hate, emotion and all the other feelings of the heroes with which the
narrator empathizes – all these were communicated to the listeners
without saying a word about them.

Our exegesis thus has the additional task of reading between the
lines to find the inner being which the narrator did not expressly
describe. This is not always so easy because we are often far
removed from the tastes of ancient times and their expression. Why
did Rebekah veil herself when she caught sight of Isaac (Gen 24:65)?
Why did Lot's daughters go to their father (Gen 19:32)? Why did

Tamar want descendants from Judah (Genesis 38)? What is the
connection between the shame awakened in the first couple and their
sin (Gen 3:7)? Earlier expositors often erred by simply assuming
modern moods and feelings. But even those who refuse to modern-
ize and make a conscious effort to search out the inner being of the
ancient Hebrew are easily subject to error. Not infrequently it will
be scarcely possible for us to come to any definite conclusion at all.

Speech and Action in the Stories

Another means by which the character of the actors is expressed
is speech. Words, though not as spectacular as actions, are for that
very reason all the better able to reveal the inner being. The ancient
storytellers were well versed in how to choose words appropriate to
the feelings of the speakers. The speech of the cunning snake reveals
its maliciousness. In the same way we discover the inexperience of
the childlike woman (Gen 3:1ff), Sarah's envy of her slave girl (Gen
16:6), Abraham's readiness to compromise (Gen 16:6), Abimelech's
righteous anger (Gen 20:9), the foresight of the clever Jacob (Gen
32:9), and the bitter complaints of both Esau (Gen 27:36) and Laban
(Gen 31:43) when deceived by Jacob. Two masterpieces of character
portrayal by means of dialogue are the story of the temptation of the
first couple (Genesis 3), and the conversation between Abraham and
Isaac on the way to the mountain (Gen 22:7-8). Speech is always
expressly introduced in Hebrew narrative, differing in this way from
the German ballad. There is a stylistic rule that avoids two successive
speeches by the same person, always interposing another's remark or
some action.

It is very striking that, contrary to our taste, the characters of
Genesis often do not speak where the present-day writer would
certainly have them do so, and where the situation seems to demand
speech. We can well imagine how Joseph was thrown into the pit
(Gen 37:24) and carried off to Egypt (Gen 37:28; cf. also 42:21) amid
loud lamentation, that a verbal exchange preceded Cain's mortal
blow (Gen 4:8), that Hagar was expelled from Abraham's house
wailing and weeping (Gen 21:14), that Isaac implored his father for
mercy in touching tones when bound on the wood (Gen 22:9). But
not a word about it! No word escaped the couple when God cursed
their life; there was no self-recrimination (Gen 3:16ff). There was

not a word from Rebekah in Gerar (Genesis 26), from Noah in the story of the flood, from Abraham when promised a son (Gen 18:10) or when ordered to sacrifice Isaac (Genesis 22). Likewise, Hagar said nothing when she saw Ishmael dying and when God heard the child crying (Genesis 21). One could easily think that the characters of Genesis were being portrayed as taciturn or even dumb. The only one ready in speech would seem to be God.

How is this peculiar taciturnity to be explained? The first explanation is that in that ancient civilization one spoke much less and more briefly than in our garrulous modern times when everyone feels the need to pour out the heart and reveal its wondrous secrets. The second is that words came less readily to the lips of the ancients, as is the case today among our peasants. This taciturnity was also due to the style of the narrators who subordinated everything else to the action. Nothing is said except that which advances the action. It was to serve this interest in particular that any description of the emotions of characters who were suffering was avoided. It would have made no difference to Joseph's fate whether he lamented or remained silent when his brothers sold him. It would have been a matter of indifference what Abraham or Noah said when God commanded them—it was enough that they obeyed. The lot of the first couple was decided when God cursed them; no self-recrimination could have helped. What more could a verbal exchange prior to Cain's mortal blow have told us? We know already why he became a murderer. It seems natural, too, that humans should normally have no reply to make to God's promises. What more can one say when God has spoken?

The other side of this taciturnity is that those speeches that the storytellers did find suitable to relate are vital to the context of the narrative. The dialogue between the snake and the woman (Gen 3:1ff) shows what led to the eating of the forbidden fruit. Cain poured out his guilt-laden heart before God who responded with a mitigation of the punishment (Gen 4:13ff). Abraham told his wife to say that she was his sister. She did, and was taken into Pharaoh's harem (Gen 12:11ff). Abraham left Lot free to go east or west, and so Lot chose the Jordan valley (Gen 13:18ff). Abraham took Hagar as his concubine at Sarah's request, and yielded again to her second request (Genesis 16). These are not superfluous speeches. Rather, they are essential in order to provide a solid basis for subsequent action. Utterances of curse and promise (Gen 3:14ff; 4:11-12;

8:21-22; 9:25ff; 12:2; 27; 28:13-14) are especially important. They are the climax of the whole narrative toward which all that precedes is directed. One can understand, too, why God was so often introduced as speaking (Gen 1; 2:16-17; 3:9ff; 4:6ff; 7:1ff; 11:6-7; 12:1ff, 7; 13:14ff; 15; 16:8ff; and many other examples), since speech is the main means by which God influences action in the patriarchal stories.

In some situations, when there was no one whom the actors could have addressed, the storytellers introduced that least concrete of all speech—the monologue (Gen 2:18; 6:7; 8:21-22; 18:12, 17ff; 26:7; etc.). God is usually the speaker in these cases; for to whom could God express his most secret decisions? In some of these cases we can deduce that there was an older form of the narrative in which God addressed his heavenly court (Gen 1:26; 3:22; 11:7).

There are, to be sure, some speeches in these brief stories which either give a character sketch of one of the actors, or provide the judgment of the storyteller, or serve some other goal, without in any way being required by the context.

Many utterances in Genesis are remarkably short. One recalls the lament of Hagar ("I am fleeing from my mistress Sarah"—Gen 16:8), or the words of Lot's daughters (Gen 19:31), of Sarah (Gen 21:10), of Abraham ("I will swear"—Gen 21:24), of Rebekah (Gen 24:18-19), of Jacob ("swear to me today"—Gen 25:33), of Isaac's servants ("we have found water"—Gen 26:32), of Laban ("indeed you are my flesh and blood"—Gen 29:14) and so on. On the other hand, ◄ speech is more prolonged in the case of the solemn and weighty pronouncements of curse and blessing. However, one can in general see taciturnity as a characteristic sign of a definite type in Genesis.

Utterances of this kind often do not represent the ultimate intentions of the actors and not infrequently allow only an indirect glimpse into their inner being. And so the words are very often not entirely clear to us and it requires special skill to explain them. The narrative tells how God forbade humans the tree of knowledge, but does not give the reason for it. What did he have in mind when he threatened immediate death and later did not carry out the threat? Likewise we hear that the snake wanted to tempt the woman, but not why. Even such psychological masterpieces as the story of the first couple's temptation provide only indirect descriptions of the psyche.

Attendant Circumstances in the Stories

The description of the attendant circumstances are just as sparse in very many of the stories. Here, too, there is a deep cleft between ancient and modern narrative style.

It goes without saying that those ancient writers were not closely attuned to the landscape; there is no trace of a feeling for nature in Genesis. The landscape may affect certain aspects of the narrative's course, but it in no way determines the mood of the action. The story of the garden takes place under green trees, thus the couple can clothe themselves with leaves. Hagar's story takes place in the harsh waste of the desert — a place where one wanders about and where there is no water. The fact that the Joseph story is set in the land of the Nile has a similarly limited impact on the narrative.

If the ancients had not lacked this awareness of the natural environment, what stimulus there would have been to give a description of the garden! Would any modern writer pass it by? But the ancient storytellers were content merely to say that beautiful trees grew there, and that it was the source of the great rivers.

Apart from this, there is no mention of the instrument with which Cain murdered Abel (Gen 4:8). Likewise, it is merely said that Noah planted the vine and drank the wine (Gen 9:20-21) without mention of the intervening process of wine-making. The story does not say how Hagar gave expression to her contempt for Sarah, nor how Sarah took her revenge (Gen 16:4-5). It is usual to admire the attendant circumstances in the narratives, and rightly so; but this is not to say that the stories abound in concrete, eye-catching details. In general, they offer little other than a variety of concrete detail. In fact the choice of such detail is so selective that we are justified in asking its purpose on each occasion. One will not find anywhere in Genesis details whose purpose would be solely graphic. Even the fact that Rebekah carried the jug on her shoulder, as picturesque as it is, had a specific purpose in the story as a whole (cf. comm. p. 254).

This sparseness of attendant circumstances is all the more striking since, in addition to details which are only hinted at, there are often other minutiae, especially in the more detailed narratives. The meal that Abraham set before the three men was described in great detail (Gen 18:6ff), whereas that given by Lot was quickly dismissed (Gen 19:3). Exegesis is much improved by paying constant attention to brevity and detail, and by asking what the storyteller had in mind.

This will reveal a rule—namely, that the storyteller portrayed concretely the main incidents but merely indicated or even omitted whatever was secondary to the action. The storyteller was very much in control here and proceeded in accordance with individual artistic judgment. For example, in the story of the sacrifice of Isaac, the three day journey was passed over, while the short walk to the place of offering was described in great detail (Gen 22:4ff). Likewise, the experiences of Abraham's servant on the single day when he was pressing for Rebekah were reported in detail. The many days he spent traveling to Nahor's city, however, were accounted for in one sentence (Genesis 24).

This emphasis on action is also evident in the way in which the stories conclude. They close immediately once the desired point is reached. There is no lengthy fade-out, just a sudden cutoff. It is important for exegesis to note this. Whatever immediately precedes the conclusion is the storyteller's climax. There are two types of conclusion: the usual type adds a further sentence to the climax to echo the emotional tone (the classic example of this is the sacrifice of Isaac, Genesis 22). The less frequent and clearly more impressive type closes with a forceful speech (for example, Noah's curse in Gen 9:20ff). [The first type is an example of the "Law of Closing," according to which, after the concluding incident, the story tempers in some way or other the emotion aroused. It is the counterpart of the "Law of Opening," according to which the story does not commence with a flurry of activity, but rises to action from a quiet beginning. The less frequent form, described above, also occurs as a new type of poetic effect in Spanish ballads. See A. Olrik, pp. 2-3; Eng. pp. 131-132.]

The Narrative Thread

We conclude, then, that in the ancient stories everything was subordinate to the action. There are narratives in other kinds of literature in which the action is merely the dress or the thread, and the main thing is the state of mind, the witty dialogue or the idea; but ancient Hebrew story was entirely different. The ancients asked their storytellers for action above all else. They wanted something stimulating to happen in the story. Now the first thing that was demanded of such an action was that it have internal unity. The storyteller had to present a closed succession of events in which one followed necessarily from the other [A. Olrik, p. 10; Eng. p. 138]. The main attraction of a story of this sort is that it shows how one thing is the result of another. The more comprehensible, the more stringent the connection, the more attractive is the narrative. A famine forced Abraham to go down to Egypt (Gen 12:10ff), but he was afraid that he would be killed there because of his beautiful wife. *Therefore* he passed her off as his sister. Deceived *by this*, Pharaoh brought Sarah into his house and gave Abraham presents. *Consequently* God struck Pharaoh, who, *as a result*, dismissed Sarah, but allowed Abraham to keep the presents. In another narrative, Sarah was barren, but wanted to have children (Genesis 16). *Therefore* she gave her maid to Abraham as a concubine. Hagar conceived, and *as a consequence* looked with contempt on her mistress. *This* offended the proud lady of the house deeply. *As a result*, Hagar ran away from Sarah into the desert. *There*, however, God took pity on her and promised her a son.

One should note how in all these stories each incident in the series is linked with the preceding, and how each preceding incident is the natural cause of (or at least presupposition to) that which follows. We usually judge this type of narrative style to be childlike. But such a judgment is only partly correct. These narratives are very closely knit. The storytellers did not like digressions or discontinuities such as abound in the narratives and epics of more highly developed literature. Rather, they moved unrelentingly and surely to their ultimate goal. "Everything superfluous is suppressed and only the essential stands out salient and striking" [A. Olrik, p. 8; Eng. p. 138]. As far as possible there is no new beginning in the same narrative, just an uninterrupted cohesion. It is very rare that anything new was presupposed. The style was to give, as far as possible, all that is presupposed at the beginning. It was the convention to omit such details which, though a necessary consequence of what had already happened, did not further the main action. On the other hand, every passage that was a necessary part of the main action had to be expressly reported. The device of guessing what has happened from speeches (which is typical of German ballads) was not used at this stage of Hebrew narrative. There was to be neither too much nor too little. In the same way the ancient story avoided dividing the overall action into a number of threads in order to develop them side by side. It "holds the individual strand fast. Folk narrative is always *single-stranded*" [A. Olrik, p. 8; Eng. p. 137].

It almost always pursued one main motif and, as far as possible, left all else aside.

In many stories the same motifs are played on in a variety of ways. The story of the garden for example ties everything to the nakedness and clothing of the couple, and has the link of "ground" (*'adāmāh*) and human (*'ādām*) run through the whole story. The story of Joseph's abduction to Egypt (Genesis 37) plays with the sleeved tunic and the dreams. The narrative of Jacob's last testament portrays vividly the peculiar actions of the dying man as he lay on his bed (Gen 47:31), as he sat up to give the blessing (Genesis 48), as he drew his feet back to die (Gen 49:33), and so on. As a rule, then, and quite contrary to our sense of style, the utterance was repeated with the event so that the same word often runs through the story like a red thread. There is frequently a whole chain of words which the storyteller constantly took up anew. Instructive examples are the two versions of the story of the deceit of Isaac by Jacob (Genesis 27, cf. comm. p. 306). This practice undoubtedly had its origins in the poverty of the language. But the storytellers whose works lie before us accepted this device because they were able thereby to put their own stamp on the unity of the narrative.

Because of this tight internal coherence of the story, it is possible in many places where our tradition has gaps or accretions to discern what was original. Our work of source division must thus often be guided by the key words in the story. Source criticism is on much firmer ground here than in the prophets, laws and songs where such tightness is missing.

It is also typical of some narratives that they often contain certain words which occur only, or predominantly, therein. As soon as one hears them, one thinks immediately of these stories (e.g., *nᵉpilîm* (giants), *tᵉhōm* (primeval deep), "ark," "flood," create," and so on). Understandably, only the oldest and most popular narratives contain such terms (comm. pp. 5, 59, 62, 67, 102-103, 119, 151, 212-213).

The Course of the Narrative

Further, the course of the narrative should be plausible, entirely credible, and indeed inescapable. The listener should at no stage be able to object that the story, either in itself or in relation to what has preceded, is improbable. Hagar had to become overbearing because she felt superior (Gen 16:4); Sarah could do nothing else but feel slighted (Gen 16:6). Certainly the plausibility at which these ancient storytellers aimed was different from ours. Their concept of nature was also different. They had no difficulty in believing that all species of animals went into the ark. They spoke of God and his intervention in a way that is more naive than is possible for us. They thought it quite natural that the snake should have spoken in the primeval period, that Joseph should have risen so quickly to the office of viceroy (Gen 41:37ff), and that he should have taken care of the sale of the grain single-handedly (Gen 42:6). We would call all this "fabulous" [*märchenhaft*; Trans.— belonging to the fairy tale], but the ancients were not at all put out by it. They were not shocked by Joseph's lack of concern for his family at home while he was in Egypt. The plausibility of the folk tale, as Olrik rightly insisted, "is always based upon the force of the internal validity of the plot; (it) is very rarely measured in terms of external reality" [A. Olrik, p. 9; Eng. p. 138]. The listener, captivated by Joseph's experience in Egypt, entirely forgot the father and brothers in Canaan.

On the other hand, events in a well told story should not be so simple as to allow one to guess the course of the narrative from the very first words. The reader would lose interest, as no one readily listens to the obvious. The storytellers described a state of affairs, developed according to their own ideas, whose ultimate outcome the listeners could not anticipate. And so they listened all the more expectantly. Jacob wrestled with a divine being. Which of the two would win? Jacob and Laban were a match for each other in cunning. Who would be able to outwit the other? The clever but noncombative Jacob had to confront the stronger but less sharp Esau. How would he get out of it (Gen 32:4ff)? Abraham had to go down to Egypt. How would he fare? There is some degree of tension in all these stories. The childlike listeners attended breathlessly and were happy when the hero was finally free from danger. The narrative was always related with the presumption that it was not yet known to the listener. "Anticipatory motifs" were not allowed. (Here we use Goethe's phrase to describe motifs that hint at a successful outcome. They are frequent, for example, in the *Nibelunglied* epic.)

The storytellers were very fond of contrasts. The child driven out into the desert became a mighty people. A poor slave languishing in prison became lord of wealthy Egypt. They took pains to force the contrasts into a single point whenever possible. In a single place, Hagar was desperate and God took mercy on her. Just as Abraham held his hand outstretched to slay Isaac, God restrained him. Lot dallied until daybreak was near (Gen 19:15ff); the next instant must bring decision. The same is true of Jacob holding fast to the divine being (Gen 32:27). Where tension is entirely absent, where there is no development, then there is no real story. Thus one should not call the creation narrative in Genesis 1 a story (cf. comm. p. 117). There was a time when this passage would have been richer (comm. p. 119), but it is now in nature no more than a scholarly construction, even though coming from a rather ancient period. Missing, too, is any real development in the many and varied little "notes" — bits of information which the storytellers passed on from popular tradition. The same is true of the stories which were fashioned out of such traditions (see chapter 4).

As we have seen the stories were not simply free, imaginative creations of the storytellers. For the most part the story was based on transmitted material which was received and reworked along with other data obtained by intuition or reflection. These presuppositions have already been treated above. It is now our task to examine the artistic handling of the transmitted material. We have thus arrived at the central point of our inquiry.

The Art of the Storyteller

As has been shown above, many of the stories answer specific questions. They were not the creation of a freewheeling, aimless imagination intent only on artistic beauty, but had a definite purpose — to instruct. If these narratives are to fulfill their purpose, then the points which are to be made must stand out clearly. They do, and to such an eminent degree that we, who were born in a time so far removed from the original basic question, can catch on to it. Any feeling reader who has accompanied Hagar on her way through the desert and shared her fortune, good or ill, will hear no word fall more soothingly on the ear than that which tells that all suffering is at an end, "God heard" (Gen 21:17). It was the storyteller's intention to give this impression, because he or she wanted to build an explanation of Ishmael's name on the words "God hears." Or what phrase in the story of the sacrifice of Isaac impresses itself so deeply on the memory as Abraham's "God will provide" (Gen 22:8) when, his heart torn with grief, he assuages his unsuspecting child. This utterance, the doing of God himself, is thus emphasized because it answers the question of the origin of the name of that place, Jeruel (God will provide). [Ed. — The Hebrew of Gen 22:8 is אלהים יראה-לו, literally "God will see to it," nearly universally translated as "God will provide." יהוה יראה appears as the place name in vs. 14. In the commentary on pp. 239-242 Gunkel argued that the original name was $y^{e}r\bar{u}$'ēl (Eng. = Jeruel, attested only in 2 Chr 20:16) and that Genesis 22 was the story of a similarly named cultic site. This name was conceived as being derived from ראה = "to see" and אל = "God." Gunkel's translation, "*Gott ersieht sich*" is the standard German translation of Gen 22:8 which nicely preserves the nuances and ambiguity of the Hebrew. It is related to the verb "to see" and means "God will choose" (a lamb), but, as with the Hebrew, with just a little stretch one can also hear "God will appear" (Scullion's translation).]

Other stories reflect historical experiences or situations. In these cases it was the task of the storyteller to allow such allusions to come through clearly enough for well-informed listeners. The actors in the story of Hagar's flight are in the first place individuals in whose fate we share; but at the high point, when God speaks about Ishmael (Gen 16:11ff), the storyteller lets us understand that the matter at issue is a people and its destiny.

Hebrew taste was particularly fond of echoing the names of the main heroes and places even when there was no intention of giving a proper explanation of them. Many stories abound in such allusions. The flood story plays on the name Noah ("rest," Gen 8:4, 9, 21), the story of the sacrifice of Isaac on Jeruel ("God provides/sees/appears," Gen 22:8, 12, 13), the story of the reunion of Jacob and Esau on Mahanaim and Penuel (comm. pp. 355-356), and so on. These stories are rich in all sorts of allusions. They are, so to speak, transparent. One who reads them quite ingenuously, simply as good stories, finds pleasure in them; but only when they are viewed in the sympathetic light of their original settings can one perceive their brilliant colors. Then they appear as glittering, twinkling works of art. What is characteristic of Hebrew popular stories in comparison to others consists precisely, unless we are mistaken, in this coruscation. A capacity and predilection for the ingenious is particularly evident in the intellectual life and literature of Israel, even to the present day.

The art of the storytellers emerged above all in that, despite the heavy underscoring of the point intended, they were able to avoid any appearance of intentionality. With amazing elegance and fascinating charm they knew how to arrive at the intended goal. They have related a short story so true to nature and so attractive that we listen unsuspectingly; and with one stroke, before we are aware of it, they have arrived at the goal. The story of Hagar's flight (Genesis 16), for example, was intended to explain how Ishmael came to be ◄ born in the desert. With this in view it sketches a picture of his father's household; and it shows how, by a completely comprehensible concatenation of circumstances, Ishmael's mother while pregnant was brought to despair and fled into the desert. So it came about that Ishmael was born a child of the desert.

In many cases the task of the storytellers was very complex. They were obliged to answer simultaneously a whole series of questions or to take up a set of presuppositions. One variant of the story of the tower inquires into the origin of the various languages and the city of Babylon. Another asks about the origin of the different localities where people live and of an ancient building. The narrative material had been passed on in the tradition in many cases (see chapter 2). There was already at hand a story of the hospitality shown by the hero to three divinities, which Israel applied to Abraham. By means of this narrative, the storytellers intended not only to give the basis for the institution of the cult in Hebron, but also and at the same time to explain the birth of Isaac and to interpret his name. The storyteller's task was to draw the different materials into a unity.

It is here in particular that these storytellers demonstrated their art. They took the main threads from the principal motif. From the secondary motifs they wove a single scene which with easy finesse they inserted into the whole. Such secondary motifs included, for example, the etymologies. A scene was inserted into the narrative of the cult of Jeruel which explained the name of the place "God provides." But this short scene, the conversation between Abraham and Isaac (Gen 22:7-8), expressed the mood of the whole so well that we could not dispense with it even if it had no particular goal at all. In other cases the artists put two principal motifs together, and in doing so created the simplest and most natural bridge between them. For example, the first part of the Hebron story spoke of the hospitality offered to the three men. The second part, which laid the foundations for the birth of Isaac, tied in with the first in the simplest way with the men engaging in a dinner conversation and using the

occasion to promise Isaac's birth. It is the most fascinating task of
the expositor of Genesis to pursue these things not only in order to
divine, as far as possible, the oldest meaning of these stories in Israel,
but also to note the subtleties of their artistic composition.
Admittedly, this amalgamation of different motifs did not always
succeed equally well. For example, in the Tamar narrative, the short
story about Tamar which was handed down and the tribal story of
Judah stand side by side, unbalanced though they are in style (comm.
p. 419). Likewise, an Israelite interpretation is rather loosely
attached to the Jacob-Esau-Laban stories.

By and large, then, the oldest stories in Genesis are not rough
narratives, carelessly thrown together. Rather, they demonstrate a
mature, sophisticated and very lively art. They are heavily "stylized."
["In summary, we find that folk narrative is formally regulated to a far
greater degree than one would think," A. Olrik, p. 11; Eng. p. 139. If
one compares Olrik's essay with what has been written above, one
will find to one's astonishment how right is his view that there are
definite "epic laws" in all folk narrative and that this has its basis in
"the common intellectual character of primitive humans," p. 1; Eng.
p. 131. Future study of Old Testament narrative will have to direct
its attention to discerning these generally valid laws. A later age
might lay its emphasis on what is characteristic of Israelite narrative
art.]

Finally, it should be further pointed out that the storytellers
scarcely ever passed an express judgment on persons or their deeds.
The narrative style of Genesis has nothing like the Homeric epithet.
By withholding their own judgments the storytellers differed
markedly from the later prophets whose influence is evident in the
way in which they reworked legend and history.   Naturally the
storytellers also had their own opinions. They were by no means
objective, but were highly subjective.   Moreover, the proper
understanding of their stories often ensues from our ability to
empathize. But they almost never gave expression to their judgment,
since they were unable to reflect clearly on what goes on in the
psyche. When such a judgment does come to the fore, it does so only
in the utterances of the actors who throw light on what has taken
place (for example, the conversations of Abraham and Abimelech in
Genesis 20 or the closing scene of the Jacob-Laban story, Gen
31:26ff).   The fact that the storytellers abstained from passing
judgment, shows that it was not a primary concern, especially among

777

the earliest narrators, to pronounce general truths. To be sure, certain truths, more or less clear, underlie many of the stories. For example, a meditation on the value of faith underlies the story of the exodus; the praise of hospitality underlies the Hebron story (Genesis 18); and the concept that the demise of peoples is due to immorality is at the base of the story of Noah's curse. But one should not interpret these narratives as if this were their real goal. They were not ideological. The situation was different with the myths which, as shown above in chapter 2, answered questions of a more general kind, and also with the later collectors, J and E [see chapters 5 and 6], who wanted to give expression to certain ideas about Yahweh and Israel, and about piety and morality (see chapter 5), but were handicapped in this by the prevailing style.

Compositional Style, Cycles of Stories

Another style developed out of the narrative style, whose essentials we have just described. This style is somewhat closer to that of the moderns, as we can discern from Genesis itself. A classic example of the older type is the story of the flight of Hagar (Genesis 16). The most obvious example of the newer one is the Joseph story. A comparison illustrates great differences between the two. The one is characteristically brief and compact, the other notably enlarged.

The most striking difference is the span of the narratives. Storytellers learned to create larger works, and they enjoyed it. A second difference is that they were no longer satisfied to narrate a single story, but were able to synthesize a number of stories into a single whole. The old inherited device of the "single strand" (see above) was abandoned and more complex action consisting of several threads was developed. This is the case in the Joseph story as well as in the Jacob-Esau-Lot and Abraham-Lot cycles.

Let us examine how these links were made. A number of related stories were at hand. This suggested that those which dealt with the same person be brought together to form a short epic, as in the Joseph and Jacob stories. The internal unity lies in the "concentration on a leading character" [A. Olrik, p. 10; Eng. p. 139] — or something similar. A number of different stories coalesced in this way, e.g., those about Lot in Sodom (Genesis 19) and Abraham in Hebron (Genesis 18). In J a creation and a garden story have been woven together (Genesis 2-3), both of which deal with the beginnings of the human race. In P the primal stories of the creation and the flood form an original whole. We note in a number of cases that the form of the link is the same—the more important story is divided into two parts and the less important is inserted between them. We call this sort of composition (which is very common in the history of literature) a "frame narrative" (e.g., *A Thousand and One Nights*, the *Decameron*, or the stories of W. Hauff). Thus the history of Jacob and Esau became the frame for the story of Jacob and Laban. Likewise, Joseph's experiences in Egypt were inserted into the story of Joseph and his brothers. The story of Abraham at Hebron was linked with that of Lot at Sodom in the same way.

In order to appreciate this compositional art, one must pay particular attention to the borders of the original stories. The storytellers usually made the transition from one narrative to another quite simply—predominantly by means of a journey. At the end of the first part of the Jacob-Esau story, Jacob set out for the east (Gen 27:42ff); there he had his experiences with Laban and then came back to Esau. In the Joseph story, Joseph's deportation to Egypt and the subsequent journey of the brothers are the binding links. Likewise the Abraham-Lot story tells how the three men first stayed with Abraham and then later on went to Sodom (Gen 18:16).

What are the reasons for these different journeys? The deportation of Joseph to Egypt was the outcome of all that had been told about him so far (Genesis 37). The journey of the brothers to Egypt was occasioned by the same famine that had already played a decisive role in Joseph's elevation in rank (Gen 42:1), and the brothers' experiences presuppose this elevation (Gen 42:6). The Joseph story, then, is a dexterously amalgamated whole.

The Jacob story is less of a unity, though here too there is an internal reason why Jacob went to Laban—he was fleeing from Esau. For the rest, the original stories stand side by side in discontinuity. [This "complete concentration" and "loose agglomeration" of the stories occurs often in folk narrative, A. Olrik, p. 10; Eng. p. 139.]

On the other hand, there is no apparent reason why the three men went directly from Abraham to Sodom. There is no inner coherence between these different stories, and so the storyteller tried all the more to create artificial links. This is why Abraham accompanied them as far as Sodom (Gen 18:16), and went back to the same place on the following morning (Gen 19:27-28). It is here that one has the clearest impression of a conscious art which strives to create a greater unity out of originally disparate materials. We find tighter links, fashioned in "frames," in the Joseph narratives. Here a whole series of narratives was compounded and woven together. Pursuing the same line, the latest storytellers arranged the whole of the material handed down: first the primal stories taking place far to the east, then the patriarchal stories localized in the east and the south of Canaan, next the Joseph stories, and finally the stories of Moses and the exodus. These stories were linked by means of migrations; so Abraham had to migrate from the east to Canaan, and the journey of Joseph's brothers to Egypt prepared for the exodus of their posterity.

A further characteristic of the Joseph story is its prolixity, by which it differs markedly from the brevity of the old narratives. We find in it a wealth of speeches, soliloquies, extensive descriptions of situations and explanations of the thoughts of the actors. The narrator was fond of repeating in the form of a speech what had already been reported. How does one judge this "epic prolixity?" It is not peculiar to this one narrative only. We find it, though less well developed, in the story of the wooing of Rebekah (Genesis 24), in the story of Abraham and Abimelech (Genesis 20), and in details of the Jacob stories (particularly in the account of the meeting of Jacob and Esau). There are parallels, too, in the narrative of the sacrifice of Isaac and in certain parts of the Abraham-Lot story.

There is obviously a new type of narrative style here, the development of a new taste, which was not satisfied, like the old, with telling the story as briefly as possible and passing over almost entirely all that is secondary. Rather, it strove for a richer presentation and more artistic development, even if the difference is marginal. In the new style there was a tendency to hold attractive or noteworthy situations as long as possible before the eye of the listener. For example, the fear of the brothers as they stood before Joseph was prolonged and the narrative deliberately proceeded as slowly as possible so that the listener had time to savor fully the flavor of the situation. Joseph did not make himself known immediately at the first meeting so that the same scene could be repeated. He had to require that Benjamin be brought before him because the aged Jacob would hesitate to comply with this command, and the moment of decision would be thus delayed. Likewise, the story of the sacrifice of Isaac proceeded rallentando up to the moment of God's intervention

(Gen 22:9-10) in order to postpone the catastrophe and sharpen the tension. "These lingering actions ... possess the singular power of being able to etch themselves in one's memory" [A. Olrik, p. 10; Eng. p. 138].

One device which was used over and again to prolong the ► narrative is that of repeating the same scene twice. Joseph interpreted the dreams of Egyptian worthies twice (Genesis 40-41), his brothers had to meet him twice in Egypt, he twice hid valuables in their sacks so as to make them afraid (Gen 42:25ff; 44:1ff), twice it is a question of Joseph's goblet, once with the majordomo and once with Joseph himself (Genesis 43-44), and so on. [This is the epic law of repetition of which Olrik speaks on pp. 3-4; Eng. pp. 132-133. The later presentation portrays the extent and significance of the matter by amplifying the individual parts. Popular fantasy, which lacks this vitality, would quickly supply the coloring. There is only one way to avoid it — by repetition. The Law of the Three, which according to Olrik is characteristic of such repetitions, and occurs very often in such cases in the Old Testament, is not found in Genesis, where the stylistic rule is that of twofold repetition.] It is normal for the two variants to differ somewhat from each other. An obviously older technique, in which the two scenes are in almost complete agreement and are even narrated in the same words, occurs only once in Genesis, in the stories of Lot's daughters (comm. p. 218). [A. Olrik, p. 8; Eng. pp. 132-133, 136.]

On a number of occasions, though certainly less frequently, the storytellers constructed new scenes on the basis of old motifs (for example, the last scene between Joseph and his brothers in Genesis 50). The inserted passage, which describes Abraham's discussion with God (Gen 18:23ff), is unique. This scene is virtually a didactic passage. It deals with a religious problem which troubled people at the time of the writer, and which was recalled while contemplating the story of Sodom (cf. comm. pp. 203ff).

These same storytellers had such a penchant for long speeches that often the action was made subordinate to them. The most prominent example is the confrontation between Abraham and Abimelech (Genesis 20). In this case, quite contrary to the rule which the ancient style followed, events were not narrated in the order in which they happened. A whole succession of events was passed over at the beginning in order to repeat them in the speeches that follow. The storyteller tried in this way to make the speeches more interesting, though at the cost of narrating the events.

A very popular device was to give content to the speeches by having one of the persons in the story narrate again what had already been reported (Gen 42:13, 21, 30ff; 43:3, 7, 20-21; 44:19ff). One of the stylistic rules in repetitions of this sort (thus differing from Homer) was to vary the second speech a little or to give it something of its own by introducing some fresh detail. This fondness for rather long speeches was, as far as one can discern, a secondary element in Hebrew narrative style, and hence a sign of a later period. And we see that precisely those passages which we recognize on other grounds as the latest growths or insertions in the story (Gen 13:14-17; 16:9-10; 18:17-19, 23-33) contain such lengthy speeches.

Other genres in Hebrew literature demonstrate this delight in prolixity. The rambling style of a Jeremiah follows the short, compact style of an Amos. Likewise there are the pithy legal maxims of the Covenant Code and the long-winded discussions of Deuteronomy; the short wisdom proverbs which form the nucleus of the book of Proverbs and the lengthy speeches which were later prefaced to it; the oldest popular songs, which are often just one line long, and the long creations of artistic poetry.

We are not altogether in sympathy with this taste of a later period. The Joseph story, for example, runs the danger of becoming far too drawn out. On the other hand, such volubility is the sign of a newly acquired intellectual power. Whereas the older period could only discuss the inner being in short, disjointed words, this later generation had learned to observe more accurately and to articulate more fully. A far higher degree of attention was devoted to the individual psyche – they had acquired both the desire and the ability to tackle psychological problems. Thus the classic example of a character portrait was created in the narrative of the sacrifice of Isaac. The narrator of the Joseph story was master of an art which made it possible to put together a picture of that man out of a number of small pieces. This narrator was particularly successful in portraying Joseph's inner emotion when he saw Benjamin (Gen 43:30), and Jacob's state of soul when he heard that Joseph was alive and was ruler of Egypt (Gen 45:26ff).

The difference between these two genres is so great that it is advisable to distinguish them by different names; the names "story" for the first and "novelette" for the second seem appropriate. The transition from one to the other is of course fluid; such transitional forms as the Laban-Jacob and the Rebekah narratives can be described as "stories embellished in the style of the novelette" or "novelettes based on (traditional) story motifs." [Ed.— Scullion's translation of *Novelle*, "short story," is much preferable to that in Carruth's translation of the first edition, "romance," but runs the risk of confusion in that an important characteristic of "short story" is that it is longer than "story." "Novella" is a precise technical term which could not be well applied to Genesis. Thus I have suggested "novelette."]

The Age of the Narrative Styles

We are now in a position to say something about the age of this style, though not without caution. The narrative art observed in the stories was later transferred to history writing, where the same or similar observations may be made. And so we see that the oldest history writing known to us follows the more detailed style. The concise style must then have been in operation for a number of centuries. But it should be noted that this determines only the age of the narrative style, not the age of the narratives preserved for us in this style.

In strongest contrast to the more detailed stories stand the very brief little "notes" which occur here and there throughout Genesis; e.g., when it is said quite briefly that Jacob met God's army in Mahanaim (Gen 32:2-3), that he bought a field in Shechem (Gen 33:18ff), that Deborah died and was buried near Bethel (Gen 35:8, 14), that Rachel died on the way to Ephrath as Benjamin was born (Gen 35:16ff), and that Sarah was buried in the cave of Machpelah (comm. p. 273). It is certainly not by chance that many of these notes mention the place where the thing happened, and that the place itself is often the main element in the whole transmission. What we must see in such bits of information are local traditions taken directly from the lips of the people. Brief place-traditions of this sort can still be heard in parts of Germany and read in story books (cf. Grimm, *Deutsche Sagen* Nos. 2, 6, 11, 12, 19, 21, 22, etc. and K. Bader, *Hessische Sagen* I, Nos. 8, 10, 11, 17, 19, 20, etc.). Later writers often constructed whole stories out of such notes.

4
THE HISTORY OF THE TRANSMISSION
OF THE STORIES IN ORAL TRADITION

The Origins of the Stories

When stories were first written down they were already very old and had a long history behind them. So by the very nature of things the origin of story is ever beyond the gaze of the scholar and goes back into prehistoric time. And so it is in Genesis as well. The great age of the stories is evident when, among other things, they often speak of peoples and tribes which have receded or become extinct, like Shem, Ham, Japheth, Cain, Ishmael, Reuben, Simeon and Levi (see chapter 2). It is further evident in the many rough and ready traits which betray to us the religion and the morality of a primal period. One has only to think of the many mythological fragments such as the story of the angel marriages (Gen 6:1ff), the story of the struggle of Jacob with the divine being, the assorted stories of lies and frauds among the founding fathers, and so on.

A number of these stories (in fact very many of them) were not produced by Israel but migrated there from foreign parts. Indeed it is the very nature of such stories, namely that they pass from people to people, from land to land and even from religion to religion. So, too, many of our German stories and tales have come from outside. Even today, modern, educated peoples exchange nothing of their cultural treasures so readily and so often as they do their stories. One has only to think of the extraordinary diffusion of modern novels in Germany. We reflect that Israel lived on soil fertilized by a civilization of thousands of years. It did not live in isolation, but was surrounded by peoples, some of whom were on a superior level of culture. (World commerce and exchange at that ancient period moved from Babylon to Egypt and from Arabia to the Mediterranean). We would thus expect that Israel's place among the

nations would be reflected in its stories, just as it is in the abundance
of foreign words in its language.

The stories show themselves to be the confluence of many
sources. They exhibit an extraordinary variety of colors. Some of
them take place in Babylon, others in Egypt, others to the east and
south of Canaan, others in Canaan itself. Some think of the
patriarchs and primal ancestors as farmers (the story of the garden),
others as shepherds. Some praise the cleverness of the ancestors
(Jacob, Abraham, Noah), but another considers the acquisition of
knowledge to be a crime against God (the story of the garden).

The Idea of God in the Stories

The idea of God in the stories is likewise varied. In one place
the divinity is bound to the night (Penuel and Sodom stories), in
another it comes forth even by day. It reveals itself in dreams, but
also moves visibly among people. It envelops the beholder of
mysteries, but the primal couple walk with it in complete trust. It
appears in fire and smoke, or without any sign at all. It dwells in the
tree, in the spring, in the stone, and seems to be no more than a local
numen, or it wanders around with the shepherd as a guardian spirit.
Its locale is the fertile land of Canaan (Cain story), but it reveals itself
to Abraham even in distant Haran; it assists the patriarchs in Egypt,
as it does in Gerar and in Nahor's city. It is involved in the minutest
household affairs, but dominates the whole world which it has
formed, and gives order to the human race (primeval story). It
scrutinizes what is most secret (Gen 38:10), but on another occasion
has to go down to the very place in order to see for itself what is
going on (Gen 11:5; 18:21). It appears in person to act and to speak,
but it also works in hidden ways, holding the threads of what is
happening secretly in its hands (Joseph story). It is merciful to the
tribal ancestor, but falls upon him by night like a murderer (Penuel
story). God is incomparably superior to human beings (Gen 24:50),
but he is concerned at their power, which is becoming all too great
(Gen 11:6), and there is even an occasion when a god is vanquished
by a man (Penuel story). Humans quietly subject themselves to
God's curse (the story of the garden), but with childlike obedience
they trust in his wisdom and goodness (Abraham's departure) and
venerate him as the protector of right (Gen 16:5; 26:22-23) and
property (Gen 38:7). Almost always (at least without exception in

the extant recensions), God is one; but there are places where there are echoes of polytheism, e.g., in the "we" of the stories of creation and the tower, or remotely in the heavenly ladder at Bethel, and in the "army" at Mahanaim. Three gods appeared originally in the Hebron story (comm. p. 200). In the Penuel story Jacob wrestles with a demon of the night—clearly a subordinate being. It is impossible that one and the same divine figure is behind all this; a variety of figures must have coalesced.

Yahweh

It is clear, too, that the name "Yahweh" was impressed upon these stories only at a later date. Nowhere (with the sole exception of the secondary chapter 15) does Genesis speak of an appearance in fire and smoke, in an earthquake, in thunder and lightning, as his appearances are described throughout the rest of the Old Testament. Moreover, there is not a single tribal or personal name composed with Yahweh. On the other hand the name El echoes from proper names like Israel, Ishmael, Penuel, and from a perhaps original Jacob-El and Joseph-El. We hear, too, expressly of El-roi at Lahai-roi (Gen 16:13), of El-'olam at Beer-sheba (Gen 21:33), of El-bethel at Bethel (Gen 31:13); El-shaddai and El-'elyon also belong to this series. Two of our collections (E and P) avoid calling the God of the patriarchs Yahweh (see chapter 5). One can see here a last remnant of a feeling that these narratives really have nothing to do with the God of the historical Israel. It is the same in the book of Job, which is clearly working foreign material and never uses the name Yahweh. Even in the third source (J), which speaks of Yahweh, at least "Yahweh ṣᵉbā'ôṯ" does not appear. It is true that some of these differences in the idea of God may be explained from developments within Israel. Nevertheless, the incredible variety can only be understood as due to the fact that the material by and large did not come from within Israel, but was extra-Israelite or at least pre-Yahwistic in origin.

Foreign Influences

In general, we may assume a Babylonian influence for the primeval stories. According to them, Babylonia itself was the original setting of the human race, and Babel the oldest city in the world. In addition, the land of Ararat is mentioned in the flood story and the rivers of the east in the story of the garden. We can demonstrate a Babylonian origin for the flood story for which we possess Babylonian recensions. The biblical creation story agrees with the Babylonian one at a very important point—the division of the primeval sea into two parts, the waters above and the waters below. The ten primeval fathers of the human race are ultimately identical with the ten primeval Babylonian kings. In particular the biblical Enoch goes back to the Babylonian figure En-men-dur-Anna (comm. p. 136). Nimrod, the king of the Babylonian cities and founder of the Assyrian cities, can be traced back to an Assyrian-Babylonian story figure. The story of the tower also deals with Babylonia and must come from that area. The Iranian parallels to the biblical story of the garden show that it, too, came from the east, probably from Mesopotamia (comm. pp. 37-38). The origin of the primeval stories explains the differences between them and the patriarchal stories, as we have seen above (chapter 2). Their universalistic attitude is due to the broader outlook of Babylonian world culture, and their stronger anthropomorphisms and their characteristically gloomier view of God are to be seen as the last vestiges of the pagan religion that once put its stamp on this material. It is also the effect of a higher culture that, whereas, according to the oldest stories about them, the patriarchs were cattle breeders, the primeval stories conceive of them as farmers (cf. Gen 8:22 "seedtime and harvest"), and speak of the cultivation of the vine, of great building projects, of cities, of towers, and of ships.

Scholars are divided in their opinions as to the time and manner in which these stories penetrated into Israel. We think it likely for internal reasons that the stories passed from people to people and had already come to Canaan and been taken over by Israel in the second millennium as it assimilated into Canaanite civilization. Canaanite influence (as well as Babylonian) is evident in the material of Genesis 1 (comm. pp. 104, 129). The figure of Noah may be of Syrian Canaanite origin (comm. p. 79). Biblical Eve may be connected with the Phoenician ḥwt (comm. p. 23), and Esau with the Phoenician "Usoos" (comm. p. 296). [Ed.—Usoos is Gunkel's rendering of the Greek Οὔσωος, the name of a Phoenician hero as it appears in Philo. This etymological relationship is discounted by modern scholars.] We know from the Tell El-Amarna letters that there was Babylonian influence in Canaan in this ancient period. A later age, when Israel's self-consciousness had awakened, would not have readily taken over such myths (comm. pp. 72-73, 128-129). It is significant that we note no sign of Egyptian influence in the primeval stories. On the other hand we suspect it (without, of course, being able to prove it with certainty) in the novelette of Joseph which takes place partly in Egypt, and may go back to Egyptian stories (comm. p. 400). Egyptian influence is especially probable in the story of Joseph's agrarian policy (Gen 47:13ff).

It is different with the stories of Abraham, Isaac, Jacob and his sons (with the exception of Joseph). The Israelite origin of the narratives which deal with these figures is, on the whole, clear. The names are expressly Israelite, as are also those in the stories of Dinah (Simeon and Levi in Genesis 34) and of Tamar (Judah in Genesis 38). The same is true of the name Reuben in Gen 35:22. These stories preserve recollections of the historical Israel which had already migrated into Canaan; they are therefore the latest in Genesis.

In the case of the stories of Abraham, Isaac and Jacob, the question must be raised whether Israel found them already existing in Canaan, or imported them when it immigrated. One should note that these narratives are set not in Canaan itself but on the steppes to the east and the south. The patriarchs of course occasionally refer to Canaan. However, it is very striking that the only information about them at Canaanite localities is in the form of "notes" (see chapter 3) or new creations; no true stories are told of them there. This is the case of Abraham at Shechem and Bethel in Gen 12:6-8 (comm. p. 167) and in Gen 13:5ff (comm. 176) and of Jacob at Bethel, Succoth and Shechem in Gen 28:10ff; 33:17ff; 35:1ff; (comm. pp. 322, 368, 378-379), and at Ephrath in Gen 35:16ff (comm. p. 382). The most significant exception is the localization in Hebron of the narrative of the three men who visited Abraham. One can clearly perceive that the narrative did not originally belong there (comm. p. 200). This leads to the conclusion that the patriarchal stories did not have their origin in Canaan, but were brought there by Israel. There was a firm recollection that the patriarchs did not belong to Canaan proper, but to the regions to the east and west. Hence, the storytellers did not generally venture to locate the narratives about them in Canaan, but were content to narrate "notes" about them at a few Canaanite places. This is because so much value was put on the patriarchs having been there first as a justification of Israel's later occupation of

Canaan. But such important places in Canaan as Jerusalem, Jericho, Dan, Shiloh, Ophrah and many others are not mentioned at all in the patriarchal stories.

A further indication that the stories about the patriarchs originated on the steppes is that the oldest narratives think of them not as farmers, but as nomads, particularly as sheep breeders. [Translator— In support of this Gunkel refers in a footnote to E. Meyer, *Geschichte des Altertums* I, 1909, pp. 305ff and H. Gressmann, *ZAW* 30 (1910):25ff, and lists the many nomadic references in the text of Genesis.] The Abel-Cain story is also in origin a story about sheep breeders (comm. p. 47), and the Cain tribal genealogy contains many names from the east and the south (comm. p. 50). The characteristic meekness and submissiveness of the patriarchs fits well with the occupation of the sheep breeder, who is constrained by the clumsiness of the animals to be peaceable. Everywhere they make treaties; and their main characteristic is astuteness, even cunning, which is far removed from the warring spirit of the later historical Israel. The nomadic situation is presented so graphically that one cannot but assume a real (though to be sure transfigured) memory of the circumstances under which the ancestors once lived. Finally, it is to be noted that the name of the Canaanite god, Baal, occurs nowhere in the patriarchal stories. H. Gressmann's surmise that the figure of El, which appears almost exclusively in the narratives of Israel's ancestors, was not taken over by Israel in Canaan, but was the god of the fathers [*ZAW* 30 (1910):28], sounds very probable (comm. pp. 187, 236, 285). Hence these stories must have been known already to the Hebrew tribes before their migration into Canaan. Precisely because of their origin these stories indirectly have great historical value.

This provides a very simple solution to one of the most important questions of Genesis—a question which has continually occupied the attention of scholars: how is it that the patriarchal story supposes a period when the patriarchs were in Canaan before Israel is known to have migrated there? The answer is: as long as it is a question of places in the Negev or the east, there are historical echoes; but when there is mention of places in Canaan proper, such as Bethel and Shechem, there is no preexistent historical tradition. It was only after Israel had migrated to Canaan from the steppes that it localized the ancestors it brought at a few places in the land. But there were not many of these places and so the view arose that

Israel's ancestors must have already been in Canaan before Moses and Joshua. It was a series of stories that arose later that projected events from Israel's historical period (after the migration) into that ancient period (comm. pp. 34, 38).

The overall picture of the transmission of stories in Israel, as far as we can discern it, is in broad lines as follows: the primeval story is essentially Babylonian, the patriarchal story is essentially of ancient Hebrew origin with some inserts from Israel's historical period, while the Joseph story is turned towards Egypt. Canaan mediated the primeval story to Israel, but had no influence on the patriarchal story as a whole. Israel was too proud to have taken over ancestral figures from the Canaanites, and too clearly aware that it was not at home in Canaan and had no ties of blood with that land.

This classification of the corpus does not come close to exhausting the entire, complicated history of the stories. It is clear in some cases (and one can suspect it in quite a number of others) that individual stories had an additional prehistory of their own, independent of these three main streams. This is likely the case for the Ishmael story which must have had its original home among the Ishmaelites. Likewise the figure of Lot would have had its setting in Moab where Lot's cave was pointed out (Gen 19:30). The story of Sodom could well have been narrated about the lava expanses of Arabia (comm. p. 216). The song of Lamech and the tribal tree of Lamech stemmed from the wild, bloodthirsty Arabian Bedouin.

Foreign Parallels

The picture becomes much more complicated when we take various parallel stories into consideration. Some of the stories and motifs coincide with Greek material. For instance, the account of the reception of the three men at Abraham's tent is told by Hyrieus of Tanagra (comm. p. 200). There are many Greek parallels to the story of "Potiphar's wife" (comm. p. 422). There are also Greek parallels to the cursing of Reuben (comm. p. 384) and the conflict between the brothers Jacob and Esau (comm. p. 294). The story of Lot at Sodom recalls those of Philemon and Baucis (comm. p. 214), and the sacrifice of Isaac recalls that of Iphigenia (comm. p. 242). There are similar parallels in the primeval stories. For instance, the contention that man and woman were originally one body (comm. p. 13) and the myth of a period of primeval bliss (comm. p. 113) were known to the Greeks, and so on. There was no immediate contact between Greeks and Hebrews in the period under consideration here, so the common material was not something native to these two peoples. It must have come to them from a great wealth of tradition that had its own home in the east. The readiest explanation of why we have discovered related stories among these two peoples is that we are well informed about them and their literature. Let us look then, though from afar, at the common narrative material of a much wider circle.

When we begin to collect parallels from the literature of the world, we encounter a formidable body of material and an immense, multifaceted picture appears. We find parallels to the stories and motifs in Genesis among the most widely separate peoples. Therefore, this is not merely a question of motifs which could arise anywhere at all. The following are examples: the earth is an egg (comm. p. 104) and the heavens a sea (comm. p. 107), creation is based on the separation of heaven and earth (comm. p. 107), a ladder reaches to the heavens (comm. p. 317), brothers murder each other (comm. p. 44), the person dying prophesies (comm. p. 308), the charm of the hero (comm. p. 135), the prohibition to look around (comm. p. 213), the water of life (comm. p. 8), people turned to stone (comm. p. 213), and very many other examples. In addition to these, there is quite a number of complete narratives which coincide remarkably with those in the Bible, and must have a historical link with them. The story of "Potiphar's wife" is known not only to the Egyptians and the Greeks, but also to the Indians, Persians, modern Arabs and many other peoples (comm. p. 422). The Sodom story belongs to a very widespread type of narrative (comm. p. 214), as does the Hebron story (comm. p. 193). The basic motif of the Joseph narrative, the maltreatment of the youngest, arrogant brother by his seniors, is common, and as a result, details of the Joseph story also recur (comm. pp. 399-400). The motif of the daughter who deceives her father and so has a child by him is likewise international (comm. p. 218), as is that of the faithful widow who, after the death of her husband, conceives a son from him (comm. p. 419). The same could be said of the innocence and fall of the first couple (comm. p. 37) and of many other motifs as well.

I have been content to collect the material in this area, to the extent that was possible, and to refrain from any further conclusions. This work needs to be supplemented and I hope that others will soon complete it. One expects that then an international study of folklore will broaden our perspective in our treatment of stories in general, that it will show the world the tremendous history of development that lies behind the Israelite material, and not least, that it will open our eyes to what is peculiar to Israel in the biblical stories.

Adaptation of Foreign Material

The foreign material was of course heavily adapted to Israelite popular taste and religion. This can be seen most clearly in the Babylonian-Hebrew story of the flood (comm. pp. 71ff). In the Israelite stories, polytheism has disappeared. The plurality of gods gave way to the one God (creation myth, comm. pp. 124ff) or were reduced to servants of the one (Hebron story, comm. p. 200). The local numina, the Elim, were equated with Yahweh and their names were considered to be additional names of Yahweh at a particular place (Gen 16:13; 21:33; 31:13, cf. comm. p. 187). Even when individual stories stubbornly resisted Israelite adaptation, e.g., the Penuel story, their appropriation and submission to the spirit of a superior religion nevertheless remains one of the most brilliant accomplishments of the people of Israel. But apart from the religious aspect, these stories underwent a number of alterations when they were taken over, of which we can survey only the smallest part. Foreign figures were suppressed in favor of indigenous ones. For example, the Hebrew Enoch took the place of the Babylonian sorcerer-priest En-men-dur-Anna (comm. p. 135). The Babylonian hero of the flood yielded to the (perhaps) Syro-Canaanite Noah, and the Egyptian stories at the end of Genesis were transferred to the Israelite figure of Joseph. There are many narratives which did not originally belong to the particular figures about whom they are now told. Again, indigenous figures were equated with foreign ones. Thus, Esau and Jacob of the stories were identified with the ancestors of the peoples of Edom-Se'ir and of Israel. This is how it happened that the representatives of the Israelite tribes Reuben, Simeon, Levi, Judah and the others were ascribed to Jacob as his sons and that Abraham, Isaac and Jacob become the ancestors of the people of Israel. Stories were also localized at a particular place. For instance, the story of the three men, known also to the Greeks, takes place at Hebron and the story of the cities that perished, which says nothing of a contemporary salt sea, is set at the Dead Sea (comm. pp. 214ff). In this way many specifically Israelite traits penetrated the stories, e.g., the prophecies: Esau (Edom) will break loose from Jacob (Israel, cf. Gen 27:40), Joseph will acquire Shechem (Gen 48:22), and Manasseh will give way to Ephraim (Gen 48:13ff). The motif of a border treaty at Gilead entered the Jacob-Laban story as a new element (Gen 31:52); and a passage about the preservation of Zoar was added to the Sodom story (Gen 19:20-23).

Convergence of Traditions

Additional changes [Ed.—or shifts] occurred as the result of exchange or by convergence of different traditions. We can suppose that this is what often happened when people met, especially on the occasions of the great pilgrimages to the tribal sanctuary, and professional itinerant storytellers came around. So the stories moved from one place to another and hence were told by different localities in the tradition that has come to us. The story of Sodom and Gomorrah was situated according to another tradition, so it seems, in Adamah and Zeboiim. According to a third tradition a similar story was told of Gibeah in Benjamin (Judges 19). The rescue of Ishmael was located at both Lahai-roi (Gen 16:14) and Beer-sheba (Gen 21:14). The meeting of Jacob and Esau on the former's return was set at Mahanaim and Penuel (Gen 32:4ff), not it seems, its original place—Esau's original home appears to have been, not in the north, but rather, in the south of Canaan (comm. p. 355). The names of the first fathers were mentioned at the different places which they were alleged to have founded: Abraham particularly in Beer-sheba (later also in Hebron and elsewhere); Isaac not only in Beer-sheba (Gen 26:23ff), but also in Lahai-roi (Gen 25:11); Jacob in Beer-sheba, in Penuel, Mahanaim, and later also in Bethel and Shechem (Gen 28:19; 32:31-32; 33:18; see comm. pp. 404, 406, 462). We will never be able to say with certainty at which place these figures originally settled; nor can we know whether Abraham or Isaac was the original subject of the Gerar story (Genesis 20; 26). These shifts are for the most part too old for us to be able to demonstrate in individual cases. The same holds true for different stories which have been joined together (see chapter 3), e.g., the garden and creation narratives of J, and the myths of creation and the period of bliss in P.

Furthermore, different figures have coalesced. The figure of Noah in Genesis consists of three originally different figures: the builder of the ark (of Babylonian origin), the cultivator of the vine, and the father of the three peoples domiciled in Syria or Canaan. The figure of Cain seems to have undergone the following history:

1) Cain, the tribal ancestor of the Kenites, celebrated because of his blood vengeance, and cursed because of his fratricide
2) was then equated with the primal blacksmith Tubal and acquired Jabal (= Abel) as a brother, and
3) was then identified with Kenan and inserted into the primal tribal tree (comm. p. 53).

Jacob according to the Esau story was the cunning shepherd who overcame the hunter. Related to him, but different, is the Jacob of the Laban story who is the clever son-in-law who outsmarted the devious father-in-law. The Joseph story presents him as the old father who has a tender love for his youngest son, with no mention of his cleverness. Jacob the strong man who wrestled with the demon at Penuel is different again; and the Jacob to whom the divinity revealed itself at Bethel is different yet again.

With the coalescence of the stories, the family tree of the patriarchs was established. Abraham thus became the father of Isaac, and Isaac the father of Jacob. Then Ishmael was made a son of Abraham and Lot his nephew, and so on. The reasons for this remain hidden from us, and there is no saying how old this family tree may be.

These modifications were accompanied by internal accommodation of the story material. This was never perfected and the stories remain a variegated world. On the other hand, one can suppose that the stories were once of very different kinds and that the process of transmission in Israel erased these differences to a considerable degree. The coalescence of the stories was a process which, in the case of the patriarchal stories, would already have been in motion before Israel's migration into Canaan. We can suppose that at the period when Israel gathered together again as a people under the first kings, it took place especially quickly and thoroughly.

The Passage of the Stories through Time

Just as the stories moved from place to place, so, too, did they move through different periods. For the most part they were retold without embellishment, often with an almost unbelievable fidelity, perhaps only half understood or utterly obscure. Nevertheless they were passed on. One understands this fidelity when one recalls that the ancients believed in the truth of these stories; when the storyteller diverged, the listeners, like our children, censured each alteration as an error. It is particularly understandable if one adds that those ancients, unlike the moderns, felt no desire to assert their right and personality by means of alterations and innovations. One can recognize how faithfully the stories were narrated when the variants of the same narrative in the different collections are compared. In the overall arrangement they often coincide word for word, despite some variations (e.g., the variants of Rebekah).

But even these stories, so faithfully narrated, were subject to the general process of change. With the coming of a new generation, with changes in external circumstances, or when people's ideas in the realm of religion, morality or esthetic taste change, popular story cannot in the long run remain the same. Slowly, surely and in steady progression the stories follow the general process of modification — some more, others less. Thus the stories offer us unusually important material for a study of the way of life of the people. One can write a whole history of the religious, moral and esthetic attitudes of ancient Israel from Genesis.

If one wants to know this history, one sets about a formal study of the variants. It is of the nature of the story and of oral tradition to exist in the form of variants. Each successive storyteller, however faithful he or she remains, and especially each particular circle and each new age, passes on the story transmitted somewhat differently.

The most important variants in Genesis are the two Ishmael stories (Genesis 16; 21:8ff), the story of the ancestress in danger which is transmitted in three recensions (Genesis 12; 20; 26) and the story of the treaty at Beer-sheba connected with it, likewise in three recensions. The variants of these two narratives were transmitted almost entirely independently of each other. There are in addition many cases in which the narratives were transmitted in the variants of J and E (or in the different hands of J) and worked together by the hand of a redactor. The main examples of this are to be found in the Jacob and Joseph stories.

There are often variants of entire stories or of individual story motifs in other biblical books. The idyllic narrative of Jacob meeting Rachel at the well (Gen 29:1ff) is told also of Moses and Zipporah (Exod 2:15ff). The renunciation of foreign gods under the oak at

Shechem is told of both Jacob (Gen 35:2ff) and Joshua (Joshua 24). Both Joseph (Genesis 41) and Daniel (Daniel 2) interpret the dreams of a foreign king.

If scholars would turn their attention first to these stories that are narrated twice or to the motifs that occur several times, they would discover certain lines of development. Then it would be possible to go further and compare stories reported only once. In such a way one can begin to see how extraordinarily varied these stories are. We have the coarsest and the gentlest, the most scandalous and the most edifying, some which reveal a very ancient, half polytheistic religion, and others which are the expression of the most exalted form of faith.

We can learn more about the history of the stories from the individual narratives. We notice there, if our gaze is focused, reworkings, either slight or extensive, which take a new direction. Furthermore, there are additions which introduce a new idea that was not in the old story (e.g., Gen 13:14ff; 18:17ff 23ff; 19:17ff; 21:11ff; 22:15ff, etc.). There are individual rare cases where we can surmise that later writers added a whole narrative to the tradition (Genesis 15). The usual sign of such additions is that they are ◄ relatively abstract—the latest are more concerned with ideas than ◄ with narrative, and so they often contain only speeches. Often short narrative "notes," which existed in popular talk mainly as local traditions (see chapter 3), were elegantly elaborated by later storytellers. This was the origin of the story of Abraham's migration (comm. p. 167), of Rebekah's marriage (comm. p. 248), of the treaty with Abimelech at Gerar (comm. p. 305), of Jacob at Bethel (comm. p. 322), and of Sarah's burial in P (comm. p. 273). The story of the birth of the sons of Jacob had a similar origin (comm. p. 330). Likewise, the narrative of the separation of Abraham and Lot is a graft on an old trunk (comm. p. 176). The second part of E's Bethel story puts together all sorts of traditions about Shechem and Bethel, and so aims at erecting a new structure out of the transmitted "rubble" (comm. p. 378). But much more frequent than the additions which these faithful storytellers made are the omissions—doing away with what has become scandalous. We see gaps everywhere in the stories (in Gen 9:22, after 12:17 and 16:14, cf. comm. pp. 192ff; the second part of the Hebron story is missing, comm. pp. 197, 199, etc.). Indeed, often so much seemed scandalous to the later storytellers, or no longer held any interest for them, that some stories have been

reduced to a torso. This is the case with the stories of the angel
▸ marriages (Gen 6:1ff) and Reuben (Gen 35:22). In other cases only
the names of the figures have been passed on without the stories
about them; e.g., the primal ancestors of the human race, Nahor,
Iscah, Milcah (Gen 11:29), Phicol, Ahuzzath (Gen 26:26), Kemuel,
Bethuel (Gen 22:21), Keturah (Gen 25:1), Adah (Gen 4:19; 36:2),
and Shaul, the son of a Canaanite woman (Gen 46:10). From the
story of the giant Nimrod we have only the proverb, "Nimrod was a
mighty hunter before the Lord" (Gen 10:9); and there is but a note
on the Horite Anah (Gen 36:24). We can see from other examples
that the stories, or particular details in them, lost their context and
were no longer correctly understood. The storytellers did not know
why it was an olive branch that the dove brought to Noah (Gen 8:11),
why Judah was afraid to give his youngest son to Tamar (Gen 38:11),
why Isaac had only one blessing (Gen 27:38), and why he had to eat
▸ well before the blessing (Gen 27:4), and so on. A sort of blue haze
lies over very many stories, veiling as it were the colors of the
landscape. We often have the feeling that we are not in a position to
restore to any extent the moods of the ancient stories, and that the
storytellers of the time no longer sensed them correctly. It is
necessary to follow up on all these observations in order to grasp the
reasons which led to such reshapings, and so to describe the internal
history of the stories. However, only a brief sketch is possible here.

The End of the Transmission

The most important moment in the history of the stories was
probably when the narratives underwent certain alterations in a later
period, when the external circumstances in which they arose had
changed. By that time no one remembered who the king of Gerar
really was (Genesis 20; 26), and it was preferable to introduce the
▸ king of Egypt (Gen 12:10ff). Or at a time when the Philistines were
in possession of Gerar, this people was introduced into the Gerar
story, something of which the oldest recensions knew nothing (Gen
21:22ff; 26). [Ed. – Gunkel has omitted a short discussion concerning
possible confusion between Egyptians and an Arab tribe with a
similar name which preceded this sentence in the first edition. "This
people" refers to the Egyptians.] The figure of Hagar, once a type of
the intractable Bedouin woman (Genesis 16), has lost the
characteristic coloring of the desert in the later period of trans-

THE STORIES OF GENESIS

mission, which was not familiar with it (Genesis 21). The stories of Jacob's dexterity with the sheep and goats (Gen 30:25ff), once the delight of knowledgeable listeners and hence spun out at length, were substantially abbreviated by later redactors for the benefit of readers whose interest they no longer held (comm. pp. 339-340). Likewise, only fragments have been retained of the theories of the gradual development of human arts and crafts (Gen 4:17ff). It is of particular significance that the storytellers enjoyed a lifestyle different from that of their ancestors. The ancestors were shepherds, they were farmers. The story has by and large remained faithful to the picture of the ancestors as shepherds (see chapter 4); nevertheless, a few (though not too many) traits which presuppose agriculture, have seeped in (comm. pp. 302, 334, 404, 464; see also the blessings Gen 27:28; 49:11-12, 15, 20). For the same reason, the "household" of Isaac (Gen 27:15) found its way into the old story which told of the rivalry between shepherd and hunter (cf. also Gen 15:3; 28:31; 33:17, and the passages about Haran, all of which perhaps belong to a secondary tradition, comm. pp. 168; 248; 325). Very often the material proper to the stories, being far from the places where it was understood, faded or was replaced by other details. This is particularly clear in the cult stories (of which more will be said below). Still more stories were forgotten because there was no longer any interest in them. In addition, the imagination, vividly aroused by such narratives, continued to work almost involuntarily.

The Religion of Genesis and the Religion of Israel

What is most important for us is the history of religion. As we have seen above, the idea of God in Genesis is extraordinarily varied. Alongside the local numina and the family god, we are aware of the far more exalted figure of the national god, and even the Lord of all peoples. It is important at this point to recall that these narratives had their origin prior to and outside of Israel. One should not without more ado explain the most profound concept of God as the oldest belief of historical Israel and then locate the primeval story's loftier image of God in a quite late period. H. Gressmann has correctly observed that the religion of Genesis is not simply the religion of Israel. One should not attribute an idea of God such as that found in the Penuel story to the oldest period of historical Israel, but to the pre- or extra-Israelite circles which contrived the narrative

[*ZAW* 30 (1910):24-25]. If, then, we want to grasp the contribution peculiar to Israel, we will have to attend, not so much to the story material itself, but to what Israel did with it, or to the process it underwent in Israel. In this regard, it is crucial to note that Israel put the stamp of its own Yahweh on the assortment of ideas about God that had been transmitted, and thereby neutralized the intrinsic differences. But however developed its own idea of Yahweh was, one can discern that it was able to embrace within it the Canaanite-Babylonian gods of the primeval stories. Hence, ancient Israel in its earliest period was able to affirm that it was Yahweh who brought the flood upon the whole world and scattered all peoples in Babel. The oldest religion of Israel therefore must have contained ideas of a universalistic kind. At the same time, however, the inferior ideas of the earlier stages of religion were not forgotten entirely; otherwise the ancient stories would have been destroyed, not transmitted. Instead, Genesis demonstrates that superior ideas struggled with inferior material and gradually reshaped it.

We note a monotheistic thrust in a great deal of the stories – an aversion for mythology, of which we have already spoken above (see also chapter 2). This attitude was continually at work in Israel with the result that narratives progressively lost their luster. We can affirm this process of withdrawal from the mythological in the creation myth, of which we possess traces of poetic variants with an older orientation (comm. p. 121). For the same reason, the flood narrative was already rather colorless in the earliest Hebrew account (J). The story of the angel marriages (Gen 6:1ff), which must have been more colorful in the older Israelite tradition, is in its present form quite mutilated (comm. p. 59). We know nothing more than the name of the *nᵉpilîm*, the Hebrew titans who, so it is said, were very famous (Gen 6:4). We can note further that the older stories speak very naively of the appearance of the divinity on earth, whereas the later period took offense at this, and brought continual refinements to divine revelation. It is very seldom that we hear in the stories of the divinity moving unencumbered among people as in the stories of the garden and the flood. It was much more characteristic of Israel to clothe the theophany in the veil of secrecy. The divinity appeared unknown to people (Genesis 18), or the ancient belief was taken up that it appeared only in the dark of the night (Genesis 19) – it revealed itself without entirely unmasking its being. Still later recensions support a subordinate divine being which J calls "a messenger of Yahweh" and E "a messenger of God." But this reworking did not happen everywhere; enough passages remain which presuppose an appearance of God himself, so that the older recensions are still apparent through the later (comm. p. 187). This same attitude led to transforming the appearance of God on earth into a revelation in a dream (e.g., Gen 20:3), or to maintaining that the messenger remained in heaven and from there spoke to the tribal ancestor (e.g., Gen 21:17). Either the secret world of the dream veiled the divinity as it revealed itself, or the divinity was not visible at all, but only heard. The final stage in this development is that group of stories in which the divinity no longer appeared at a definite place in the account, but remained hidden in the background as the ultimate director of all, as in the cases of Rebekah and Joseph. There is, then, in Genesis a progression in several stages from crass mythology to a belief in providence which is quite modern and acceptable to us. It is truly surprising that the Penuel story (Gen 32:25ff) was transmitted in so primitive a form. It was utilized while leaving in the dark the real identity of the god who attacked Jacob.

Cult Stories

We note, with the gradual refinement of revelation, how the link between the cult places and the divinity was loosened. The belief presupposed in the cult stories, that the god belonged to a particular place and could only be effective there, is not clearly evident in any of the stories of Genesis. The attitude of the stories in their Israelite version is rather that the places are holy to the divinity because once in the primeval period it appeared to an ancestor. Even the ancient Hebron story, which still allows the divinity to eat (Gen 18:8), no longer narrates that it appeared from a tree. In the story of Hagar's flight the ancestress meets the god at the well (Gen 16:7), but the relationship between the god and the well is left in the dark. How old this whole development is can also be seen in the Bethel story. Very ancient religion looked for the god of the place in the stone, as the name of the holy stone (beth-el = house of god) shows; but the one Israelite recension of the story affirms that the divinity lives high above Bethel in heaven. Only a ladder connects God's real dwelling and its symbol. But this belief in the heavenly house of the divinity comes from a very ancient period, as the originally mythological picture of the heavenly ladder shows (comm. p. 322).

▶   Many cult stories have come down to us in a very faded form. In
the Ishmael story (both recensions, Genesis 16 and 21), as well as in
the stories of Hebron (Genesis 18), Mahanaim (Gen 32:1ff), Penuel
(Gen 32:25ff) and others, we no longer hear a word of these places
being used as places of worship. The story of the sacrifice of Isaac
(Genesis 22), once a cult story, no longer has any etiological purpose
▶ in the received recension — it is only a character portrait. The
anointing of the stone at Bethel (Gen 28:18), rather than a sacrificial
action, seems, in its present form to be some sort of consecration rite.
The *maṣṣēbōt*, once holy stones and symbols of the divinity, are now
but simple memorial stones or tombstones (comm. pp. 320, 352, 381).
The cave at Machpelah, formerly the residence of a goddess [H.
Gressmann, *ZAW* 30 (1910):6], is in our narrative only the burial
place of the ancestress (comm. p. 274), and so on. One perceives
from the faded form in which these sanctuary stories are retained
that, in certain circles, the sanctuaries were at that time on the point
of receding from the foreground of religious interest. The bond
between sanctuaries and religion was already loosened for many
when the passionate polemic of the prophets cut it completely. How
else would the people of Judah have put up with "the deuteronomic
reformation" which destroyed these places, with the exception of the
royal temple in Jerusalem (2 Kings 23)!

God and the Individual

Genesis also has a great variety of statements about the
▶ relationship of God to humans. Some individual stories, preserved in
a particularly ancient form, give no thought at all to human moral or
religious conduct in such divine dealings. God revealed himself to
Jacob in Bethel simply because Jacob came to Bethel. Likewise, the
divinity attacked Jacob at Penuel without any apparent reason. God
took pleasure in Abel's offering because he liked Abel as a shepherd;
he enjoyed Hagar's stubborn pride; he protected Abraham in Egypt
and saw that the patriarch's lie redounded to his good. Jacob
acquired Isaac's blessing by lies and frauds. In a conflict of one
patriarch with another, God took the part of his favorite, even when
the latter was clearly in the wrong, as Abraham with Abimelech (Gen
20:7), or when the favorite acted deviously, using quite dubious
means (Gen 30:25ff), and so on.

However, there are also stories on a higher level according to which God made his grace dependent on the righteousness of humans. He destroyed rebellious Sodom, but spared Lot because of his hospitality. He killed Onan because of his impiety (Gen 38:9-10), and expelled Cain because of his fratricide. He came to Joseph's aid because he showed himself worthy by his chastity and magnanimity. He gave Abraham a son because of his friendliness to strangers (Genesis 18). These stories, taken as a whole, belong to a later, morally attuned period. But they were very old in Israel. The belief that God looks with favor on the just one, but repays the rebellious according to his or her guilt, was from time immemorial a trait of the religion of Israel (e.g., 1 Sam 24:20; 2 Sam 3:39).

In a broader sense one might add another group, namely stories that tell of God's mercy to the suffering and despairing. He assisted the despised wife (Gen 29:31), he rewarded the peacemaker (Gen 13:14ff), and brought the guiltless Joseph out of prison. This divine attitude finds particular expression in the story of the expulsion of Hagar (Genesis 21).

A third type of story lays special emphasis on what it is that wins God's favor: it is faith, obedience, and unshakeable trust that God reckons as righteousness. Noah built a ship on dry land at God's command (comm. p. 61); Abraham left the security of his homeland and, at God's word, went into foreign parts; he trusted in the promise that he would become a people, even though he did not yet have a son (Genesis 15). The story of Rebekah (Genesis 24) shows how such a steadfast trust in God finds its reward. In the story of the sacrifice of Isaac (Genesis 22) a wonderful character portrait is sketched of how the truly pious person submits to the most difficult and fearful trial because God orders it. The famous prayer of Jacob (Gen 32:10-13) presents the humble gratitude of the pious man who finds himself unworthy of the divine favor. The narratives and passages which speak of faith in this way constitute the zenith of the religion of Genesis; these are what primarily give the book its value, even for present-day devoutness. But there is no doubt that these are all later constructions. For most of them, one can demonstrate that this judgment is correct from other evidence as well. The Babylonian recension of the flood story knows nothing of the testing of the hero's faith. Jacob's prayer is secondary in its content (comm. pp. 356ff), and how remarkably does this deeply sensitive prayer rise above the conduct elsewhere of the elusive Jacob. And how markedly does it differ from the story that follows immediately, where Jacob is in physical combat with the divinity! The story of Abraham's migration is a late construction from older "notes" (see above), and the story of God's covenant with him (Genesis 15) is a new formation without any ancient tradition!

Hence we can trace a line from the less refined to the loftiest ideas about God. Genesis mirrors the struggle that this loftier religion fought for Israel's soul. In any case "the most original form of the Yahwism of the patriarchal stories is in its moral orientation, high above the attitude of other religions which allow the gods to oppose in unsavory manner all that the ethic of the time demands of humans" (E. Haller, *Religion, Recht und Sitte in den Genesissagen*, 1905, p. 42).

Furthermore, the patriarchal stories show that it is an error to think that ancient Israel was conscious only of God's relationship to Israel. Rather, the talk is always of God's attitude to the individual. Admittedly these persons are to some extent racial stereotypes, but the stories understand them as persons and describe God's attitude about them in the way in which it was thought at that time that God dealt with individuals. To misunderstand this would be to rob many of these narratives of all their attraction. The Hebron story (Genesis 18) was so gladly heard by ancient audiences because it tells how God rewards hospitality (yours and mine!). Likewise, the narrative of God listening to the voice of the crying boy Ishmael (Gen 21:8ff) is so touching because in it God takes pity on a child; this God will also listen to the crying of our children!

We recognize another line of development in that in the older stories secular and religious motifs are mingled, obviously without embarrassment or scandal. And so the story of Abraham in Egypt glorifies the cleverness of the patriarch, the beauty of the ancestress, and the fidelity of God (Gen 12:10ff). The flood story praises not only Noah's piety, but also his astuteness (in the passage about sending out the birds, comm. p. 64); and the story of Hagar's flight (Genesis 16) gives a realistic account of the situation in Abraham's household and of God's intervention. These stories therefore had their origin in a period when the secular and the spiritual worked together, when Israelites fought at the same time for God and the popular hero ("a sword for Yahweh and for Gideon" Judg 7:20), when robust humor was still compatible with piety. One only has to think of the merry slaughter by Samson, who is at the same time a

man dedicated to God, and the humor of the story of Abraham in
Egypt (comm. pp. 172-173). It can be seen from the variants,
especially of the Abraham story (Genesis 20 and 26; comm. pp.
225-226), that this mingling of secular and religious motifs was no
longer tolerated by a later period, which at the very least considered
it offensive to it to glorify simultaneously God and the secular
qualities of humans. This period therefore shaped stories which are
"spiritual" in the real sense, i.e., they deal only with God and
devoutness, leaving the secular motifs in the background. Stories of
this sort include Abraham's migration (Genesis 12), the making of
the covenant (Genesis 15), the sacrifice of Isaac (Genesis 22), and so
on. The popular story was at this point on the verge of becoming
"legend"; i.e., "spiritual" narrative.   ◄

The older period was also familiar with patriarchal stories of a
purely secular nature, such as the story of the separation of Abraham
and Lot (Genesis 13), or of Jacob and Laban. But these worldly
stories are on the whole well in the background, and much religious
material found its way into them in the later process of transmission.   ◄
For example, offense was taken at Abraham's acquisition of Canaan
simply because Lot did not want it; and so we have the insertion that
God himself promised Abraham the land again after Lot had gone
his way (Gen 13:14-17). There are reservations about narrating that
Jacob fled from Laban, and so there is the interpolation that God
suggested the plan to him (Gen 31:3). If we compare the overall
impression of Genesis with other great groups of popular stories such
as the Homeric poems or the *Nibelung* cycle, we recognize clearly the
overwhelming predominance of religious thinking in Genesis. One
can indeed doubt that ancient Israel itself was from time immemorial
so "spiritual." Rather, there would have been particular "spiritual"
circles from which we have received the popular story (see chapter 5
below).

The Stories and Morality

One can read a whole history of morality out of the stories. Very
many of them are the result of the joy taken in the figures of the
patriarchs. In a variety of ways this era, which first told the stories to
itself, shows that it has no reservations about those things which we
find shocking in the patriarchal figures; rather, they are an occasion
of pleasure or delight: "Abraham was the great father of a multitude

of nations, and no one has been found like him in glory" (Sir 44:19). The ancient people took pleasure in Benjamin living on plunder (Gen 49:27), in Hagar's stubborn courage (comm. p. 192), in the resoluteness of Tamar (comm. p. 415ff) and Lot's daughters (comm. p. 218) who had union with a man where they found one, in Abraham's clever lie in Egypt (comm. p. 170), in Joseph's astuteness when he introduced his brothers to the king as sheep breeders (Gen 47:1; comm. pp. 464ff), in Rachel's cunning in deceiving her father in such a masterly way (Gen 31:34; comm. p. 348), and particularly in the intrigues and tricks of that arrant knave Jacob (comm. pp. 298-299, 307-308, 310, 337, 366). It is impossible to overlook the role played by cunning and deceit in the patriarchal stories. The more ancient period enjoyed it so much that it appears characteristic to us. We note many examples where a later tradition was scandalized and recast or reshaped the stories, trying as much as it could to remove what was offensive. This is most obvious in the variants of the story of the ancestress in danger. Later writers reworked the whole story, which they found highly offensive, turning Abraham's lie into a mental reservation (Gen 20:12), recasting the insulting presents which the patriarch received for Sarah into a vindication of his honor (Gen 20:16), and ultimately deriving his wealth from Yahweh's favor (Gen 26:12ff); further, Abraham's deportation (Gen 12:20) has been changed into its opposite (Gen 20:15; comm. p. 225). The stubborn Hagar (cf. Genesis 16) became the unhappy, suffering wife in Gen 21:8ff so that God's mercy to her might not give offense (comm. p. 232). Abraham's conduct towards Hagar was explained by adding that God ordered him to drive her out (Gen 21:11ff). There was a special attempt to purge Jacob's conduct towards Laban of disrespect. In several long speeches the narrator advanced proof that no shadow lay over Jacob. Jacob's wives, and finally Laban himself, had to acknowledge that justice was on Jacob's side (Gen 31:4ff, 36ff). The tradition also ascribed to God's providence that which might appear suspicious to humans (e.g., God always made the herds reproduce to Jacob's benefit, Gen 31:7, cf. comm. p. 342). The narrators intervened less forcibly in the Tamar story; but here, too, they tried with all their might to whitewash Judah. They emphasized, among other things, that Judah only went to a temple prostitute after his wife died (comm. pp. 414ff). Likewise, the tradition was very concerned to treat Lot gently in the scandalous story about his daughters—he was tricked by them (comm. p. 219).

The ancient period certainly enjoyed the patriarchs, but it did not hold them up as saints. Unashamedly, it told all sorts of stories about them which are not at all edifying. Some of the old narratives are "rough hewn"; they portrayed the patriarchs as old popular types, just as people actually are. For the most part, the figure of Abraham embodies that which is ideal—faith, peace and righteousness. Yet, even about him we hear some things which are not at all ideal, but downright human. The story of Hagar's flight sketches the people in Abraham's household (Genesis 16): Sarah as the jealous wife, Hagar as the stubborn slave woman, and Abraham as the accommodating husband. But the later, "spiritually" sensitive period did not tolerate this. It saw the patriarchs as models of piety, and indeed the very heightened, delicate piety which was this generation's possession. Thus the portrait of Abraham lacks harmony. The same Abraham who expelled his son Ishmael to suffer misery (Gen 21:14), who had no misgivings about handing over Sarah to the foreign king and receiving presents in return (Gen 12:10ff), is the one who is the lofty example of faith for all time! Likewise, the cunning Jacob utters a marvelous prayer of thanksgiving (Gen 32:10ff)! We dispel this discord and we free the stories from the horrible suspicion of untruthfulness when we recognize that the different melodies come from different times.

The ancient period also had no reservations about making the right of foreigners yield in favor of the patriarchs from time to time; so Pharaoh's right became Abraham's (Gen 12:18-19), and Esau's Jacob's (Gen 27:36). To be sure, some of the fathers were simply given up—Simeon, Levi and Reuben were cursed by the primal ancestor (Gen 49:3-7)! Israelite patriotism at that time was still sound enough not to take offense. But the later period, with its heightened, one-sided respect for the "people of God," did not tolerate any suggestion that the fathers could have done wrong. Hence one notes that one of the narrators is at pains to show that Abraham was not entirely in the wrong with respect to Abimelech (the speech in Gen 21:11-13, E, comm. p. 223). For the same reason, namely that nothing offensive is to be narrated about the fathers, only a fragment of the story of the cursing of Reuben has been passed on (Gen 35:21-22), and there have been a number of attempts to rework the story of Simeon and Levi (Genesis 34). First they tried to find grounds for excusing the brothers in that they were defending the honor of their sister (J). In the end, the brothers were justified

86 The History of the Transmission in Oral Tradition

and their betrayal of Shechem was represented as quite natural. Here, too, God ultimately has to side with them (E, comm. p. 373). Such reworkings do not always please us, and it often seems to us that they made matters worse rather than better. Such is the case with the lie of Abraham, who passed his wife off as his sister. The ancient people appreciated the cleverness of this lie, and indeed it was more tolerable than the mental reservation which was substituted for it (Gen 20:12) and which appears to us "jesuitical." Nevertheless, this should not be cause to forsake our delight in the gradual refinement of moral judgment which we see in Genesis.

The Spirit and Flavor of the Stories

In the preceding chapter we have already dealt with the history of esthetic taste to be discerned in these stories. What follows is by way of appendage. One could look deeply into the heart of this ancient people by listing the main motifs the narrators particularly liked. But we shall not do that here. Let us only mention briefly how little talk there is of murder and war (see above). This is in marked contrast to the old Germanic stories where combat and war are the things that occupy men's lives and which are narrated about them. Genesis, on the contrary, speaks of peaceful undertakings and household matters, and particularly of the begetting of children. Eating and drinking also play a major role. The storytellers have firsthand knowledge of the lives of the shepherd and farmer and hence are a primary source for our "archaeology"; they are not experienced in political matters, but remain rather on the level of popular naïveté. The happy optimism that runs through the patriarchal stories is significant: "offensive situations are avoided as far as possible, and all critical situations are resolved easily and quickly" (E. Haller, op. cit., pp. 39-40; cf. Gen 12:17ff; 16:7ff; 21:17ff; 22:11ff; 38:25ff; 41:1ff); Yahweh, too, is predominantly the gracious protector and helper. Thus the stories have an idyllic coloring, even those which one is accustomed to calling "patriarchal." The more serious side of the idea of God is more evident in the primeval story; but here, too, the gloomy mood of paganism is dissipated or alleviated by reflections on the righteousness of God's judgments or on his grace, which continues to watch over the just and have mercy on the sinner.

The older stories are often quite earthy. One only has to think
of the stubborn Hagar (Genesis 16), or how Jacob, to the delight of
the listeners, deceived his blind father (Genesis 27), or how Laban's
witty daughter outwitted her father (Gen 31:33ff). It must have been
a robust generation that took pleasure in such stories. Later
narratives, however, are quite different, overflowing with tears, such
as the story of Hagar's expulsion (Genesis 21), the sacrifice of Isaac
(Genesis 22), and especially the Joseph stories. A new generation
expressed itself here, one that loved emotion and tears. There is also
another difference between the older and the later period. The
former most enjoyed well known matters of the immediate
environment, while the latter sought to give its narratives the appeal
of foreign matters by having the story take place far away and by
interspersing descriptions of foreign customs; e.g., the Joseph story.
Likewise the old stories had their characters act just as people act;
any wife would react to the insolence of the concubine (Gen 16:5),
and any good brother would avenge the shame of his sister (Gen
34:7). But the later style found any deviation from the usual worthy
of note, e.g., the way in which Rebekah was taken home by her
bridegroom contrary to all customs (Gen 24:61ff), or how the dying
Jacob made his act of reverence not on the floor but on the bed (Gen
47:31).

Stories: How Old and Late?

Consequently, we have plenty of yardsticks by which we can
measure the age of the narratives. In fact, we are often in a position
to describe the whole prehistory of a particular story, as in the Hagar
story of Genesis 16, where first an El, then Yahweh himself, and then
his messenger have become the God who appears (comm. pp.
187-188). Often a series of different reasons lead to the same
conclusion about the age of a story. There are, for example, many
reasons for maintaining that the story of Abraham in Egypt (Genesis
12) is very old: it is very short, has an ancient local coloring and does
not idealize the figures. On the other hand, there are many
indications that the Joseph story is very late: it exhibits the very late
and very diffuse style, has very few etiological traits, and contains the
belief in providence. It quite often happens that different
considerations are in opposition. The story then may be a checker
pattern of the old and the late. For example, the narrative in Genesis

15 is relatively late since it lacks embarrassing complications, but the theophany in fire and smoke is certainly a very ancient image. Thus individual developments are not neatly segregated. What is older has often persevered a long time, so we should not think of the history of these stories as simple and rectilinear, but as checkered and varied. An overview of the complete history of these reworkings forces us to admit that we can perceive with certainty but a small part of the entire process. These transformations would have been going on for a long time, and were already at work in a period into which our sources do not permit us to look. We must be warned therefore not to be too hasty in wanting to establish the primal meaning of the stories.

The Names in the Patriarchal Stories

[Translator — Throughout this section Gunkel refers constantly in the text and in footnotes to E. Meyer, *Die Israeliten und ihre Nachbarstämme*, 1906, and H. Gressmann, "Sage und Geschichte in den Patriarchenerzahlungen," *ZAW* 30 (1910):1-34.]

If it is scarcely possible for us to determine from our sources the primal meaning of all individual stories, then we must approach with great caution the question of who the figures in the patriarchal stories were. Some of them are actually names of peoples, tribes and cities, like Cain, Shem, Ham, Japheth, Canaan, Ishmael, Ammon, Moab, Shechem, Hamor, and the tribes of Israel. Israel and Edom are of course also names of peoples; however, it is worthy of note that the ancient story does not use these names, but rather Jacob and Esau. "Israel" and "Edom," therefore, are not original figures in the stories. An inscription of Thutmose III (15th cent.) mentions a central Palestinian city or region *y'qb'ar*, which would correspond to the Hebrew *ya'qob'el* (Hebrew "l" = Egyptian "r"); the name *yaqob-'el* would be related to Jacob as *yiphtah-'el* and *yabne-'el* are to Jephthah and Jabneh. One might also compare the tribal and place names Israel, Ishmael, Jerahmeel, and Jezreel (cf. E. Meyer, pp. 281-282). Nevertheless, it would be precipitate to conclude that the biblical figure of Jacob goes back to this Canaanite *yaqob-'el*. Similar formations with *'el* are found very often in south Arabic and west Semitic names of the time of Hammurapi. In particular *yaḥqub-êl* (Jaqubum) is attested as a personal name (cf. H. Ranke, in H. Gressmann, p. 6). Furthermore, the basic material of the Jacob stories in Genesis is not original to the land of Canaan. Asher has also been equated by some scholars with a Syrian regional name, *'y-s-rw* (Aser), found in inscriptions of Seti I and Ramses II (ca. 1400 BCE). Likewise, Joseph has been equated with the Canaanite city name *yšp'r*, which is mentioned by Thutmose III. However, it is to be noted that many other names, in particular Abraham, Isaac and those of all the ancestresses, are not tribal names. Moreover, to assert that some of the figures bear the names of peoples is by no means to say that most of what is related abut them, or even just the overall picture of them as individuals, is to be explained from the fortunes of these peoples. Very much of what is reported about such a popular hero may have been applied to that person later, as is clear in the case of Joseph (see chapter 2). *The interpretation of the figures in Genesis as people is not a master key which opens the way to understanding them.*

It is equally fruitless to explain them as onetime deities. There are some figures which could have originally been gods. One example might be Gad, the god of fortune, but it should be noted that Gad also occurs as a personal name. The name Obed-edom, "servant of Edom," seems also to go back to a god of Edom who perhaps appears elsewhere as well. Jeush, the name of a family in Edom, is the Arabic name of the god *yaghûth*; and a Sabaean god *qainân* is attested. The classic example of the coincidence of the name of the god with that of the political unit would be "Ashur," at the same time the name of the people and of the god. Other divine names have also been conjectured: *šelaḥ* (Methuselah = man of *šelaḥ*, comm. p. 156), *reʿu* (the name *reʿyʾel*, comm. p. 156), Nahor (it has been discovered as the name of an Aramaean god, *naḥar*, comm. p. 156), Terah (perhaps the north Syrian god *tarḥu*, comm. p. 136), and Haran (cf. the name Bethharan = temple of Haran, comm. p. 158). "Sarah" and "Milcah" were, as we know, names of goddesses of Haran, and the biblical figures of Sarah and Milcah could be linked with them. The name of Laban, too, may recall that of a god, *leʾbana* (= moon, comm. p. 163). The question has also been raised whether Joseph might be an old Canaanite god (but this seems to be very dubious). Earlier, and again more recently, there has been a constant attempt to explain the figures of Abraham, Isaac and Jacob as being originally gods. To be sure, Isa 51:1-2; 63:16 and Jer 31:15 seem to point to a cult of the ancestors at the grave of the patriarchs Abraham, Israel, Sarah and Rachel, as is still the case today in

Hebron. But it could well be that the Israelite figure has taken the place of some former divinity (comm. p. 274). As B.D. Eerdmans (*Alttestamentliche Studien* II, 1908, p. 7) rightly points out, even today in the Muslim east, historical persons are venerated as saints at their graves. The cult name *pahad yiṣḥaq*, "the Fear of Isaac" (Gen 31:42), is no proof at all of a god Isaac; as the parallel "the God of my father" clearly demonstrates. The name of the god is not "Isaac" but "the Fear of Isaac," i.e., the God before whom Isaac is in awe, as "the Holy One of Israel" is the God whom Israel holds as holy (comm. p. 349-350). There have been attempts to establish a god named Jacob by recourse to a Hyksos king, *y'pq-hr* (= "[the god] Jacob is satisfied"); but the reading is uncertain. E. Meyer (pp. 267ff), following P. A. de Lagarde's suggestion, equated Abraham with the Nabataean god Dusares, explaining the latter as *dû-šarâ*, i.e., the husband of a goddess *šarâh*; but it remains questionable whether the second part of the name Dusares is really a goddess, or perhaps just a region. The suggestion that some of the patriarchal figures might be displaced deities cannot be sustained in the most important cases — Abraham, Isaac and Jacob. Moreover, Jacob and Abraham are attested as common personal names in Babylonian. They were thus probably never anything else than names of human beings.

The Patriarchs and Myth

It is of particular importance that the stories are not full of all sorts of mythical echoes. Rather, there are but very few elements which can be so explained. It seems that Joseph's dream, in which the sun, moon and eleven stars must prostrate before him (Gen 37:9), was originally an oracle concerned with the lord of heaven, before whom the highest heavenly powers bow. But this dream, so it appears, was only inserted into the Joseph story later (comm. p. 405), and is no evidence at all that Joseph was the supreme lord of heaven. Jacob's encounter with the divinity has often been explained as Jacob being conceived of as a semi-divine giant (comm. p. 361), but H. Gressmann (p. 20) shows that an encounter with a demon can also be narrated of a human being. And the conjecture of H. Winckler, earlier repeated also by the author, that the 318 servants of Abraham are really the 318 days when the moon is visible during the year, is quite uncertain, because the number 318 is not attested in the East (comm. p. 283-284). The assumption that the patriarchs are humanized deities will always remain probable as long as one proceeds from the general presupposition that story arose out of myth. But now that this theory has disintegrated, and that scholars are beginning to see the basic form of narrative in the "(folk) tale," which also speaks of human beings, one should also be inclined to acknowledge that the patriarchs, too, are none other than human beings. At any rate, we must in the future demand from those who explain the stories of Genesis from mythology a far greater precision than we have so far found. Henceforth, it will not be enough merely to explain individual elements in a story as mythical. Rather, we require that it be demonstrated to us that entire stories bear striking resemblances to myths that have been preserved, or that the stories can be quite clearly understood as originally myths. Scholars have not yet succeeded in advancing such proof. And we must further ◄ demand that those scholars who want to recognize some mythical basis for these stories first of all study as accurately as possible the obvious history of these stories from the sources available to us. Without such previous esthetic analysis of the stories, all this scholarship remains up in the air.

The Patriarchs and History

Even though we maintain that figures like Abraham, Isaac and Jacob are real persons without any original mythical basis, that does not at all mean that they are historical. They are no more so than Brünnhilde and Siegfried, whose names are also personal names. It is difficult to comprehend the significance of the opposite view — that of the "apologetes" for religion and its history. For if there were once a man named "Abraham," and this is their assumption, then anyone who knows the history of stories is certain that the story is not able to preserve a portrait of Abraham's personal piety over so many centuries. The *religion of Abraham" is really the religion of the storytellers, which they ascribe to him.* H. Gressmann (pp. 9ff) has magnificently described how one should conceive the origin and growth of figures like Abraham and Jacob. There was, and this is more or less assumed, a primal narrative, perhaps that of the visit of the three gods to an old man which, in accord with this type of narrative, and like modern "(folk) tales," mentioned a particular, and at that time popular, name. Other suitable material was then applied to the figure of "Abraham." But the decisive step to our "Abraham" took place when Israel appropriated this developed figure as its ancestor. The original Jacob may be the astute shepherd Jacob who deceived the hunter Esau. Another story of the deception of the father-in-law by his son-in-law was all the more easily added as both were shepherds. A third cycle of stories of an old man who loves his youngest son was transferred to this figure, and this youngest son, at a time when Jacob was equated with Israel's ancestor "Israel," was called Joseph, and so on. Our conclusion therefore is the following: *the most important of the patriarchs are figures of poetic imagination.* The historical value of these figures consists in the historicity of the situations described in the stories about them, and their religious-moral value in the ideas that these narratives express.

5

YAHWIST, ELOHIST, JEHOVIST
THE OLDER COLLECTIONS

Collectors and Writers

The collection of the stories had already begun in the oral tradition. We have previously described (chapter 3) how individual stories first came together, and were finally formed into larger groups. These collectors also constructed linking passages, a particular example being the story of the birth of the sons of Jacob (Gen 29:31ff). This is not a popular story, but a creation of the ancient storytellers and must have already been in existence before J and E (comm. p. 330). By recording the stories, the process of collecting was continued and the entire tradition of the ancient narratives brought together. To what extent the main groups, now extant in our present Genesis, were already in existence in the oral tradition is difficult to say; but it seems certain that these groups (i.e., the primeval stories, the patriarchal story, the history of Joseph and the narrative of Israel's exodus which follows it) were first joined together when the collections were put in writing. This consigning of popular traditions to writing would have taken place at a period which was particularly disposed to writers, and when there would have been concern that the oral tradition could die out if it were not fixed in writing. One can perhaps conceive that it was a time when the guild of storytellers had, for reasons which we do not know, ceased to exist. This fixing in writing would in turn have contributed to the death of the still extant remains of the oral tradition, just as the written law killed the institution of priestly torah, and the New Testament canon the early Christian enthusiasts in the Spirit.

The written collection is not the work of a single hand nor did it take place at any one time; it was a long drawn out process, and the work of many. We can discern two periods in this process: the older,

94   Yahwist, Elohist, Jehovist

to which we owe the collections of the Yahwist (J) and the Elohist
(E), and the later, a thorough reworking by what is called the priestly
school (P). In what we have said so far, we have used in substance
only those stories known to us from J and E. All these written
sources contain not only the stories of the beginnings, but also
narrate histories in broader perspective, the theme of which has been
described as "the election of Israel as Yahweh's people" (G.
Wildeboer). However, the following discussion will deal with the
histories only in so far as they are relevant to the book of Genesis.

The distinguishing between these three written sources in
Genesis is the communal result of some century and a half of Old
Testament scholarship. Since the awakening of the modern
Protestant scholarly approach to the Bible, critical questions
regarding Genesis have received preferential treatment. There has
been an astounding amount of industry, critical acumen, and
ingenuity devoted to this work; and the result is something of which
posterity can be proud. In many cases one can now determine which
verses, indeed even which words, belong to which sources, even
though much still remains unclear. The last decisive move in the
history of the critical study is due to J. Wellhausen. In his masterly
Prolegomena to the History of Israel, he expounded how to determine
the sources of Genesis chronologically and to insert them into the
overall course of the history of the religion of Israel. A very recent
segment of criticism has shown that the written sources J, E and P
themselves go back to subsidiary sources. K. Budde has demonstrated this for J in his *Urgeschichte*, 1883.

Sources and their Tributaries

How is one to judge the literary type of the "sources" J and E
and their tributary sources? First, one must concede in general that
these writings rest on oral sources and that they are collections. But
one can conceive of several types of "collections" of this sort. There
are collections which have been arranged by individual writers who
aimed with full deliberation at reworking into a unity the varied
material that came to them, and so interpreted it as to impress their
own personal stamp on it. There are also collections which, as it
were, came together spontaneously, without such deliberate
reworking by individuals, and in which the pieces that came down
hang together loosely, without showing any rigid unity. It is obvious

that these two types of collections must be handled very differently. In the first, it is the writer who must be explained, in the second the received material itself. How, then, is one to judge the sources J and E and their tributaries? Current scholarship is generally more inclined to stress the individual writers behind them. Scholars have tried to derive a unified picture of the authors from the different data in the writings, and have often put the main emphasis on the writers, giving secondary import to the character of the writings as collections.

On the other hand, two things must be pointed out. First, these writings are not very homogeneous, but contain very different sorts of material. J consists of individual stories (e.g., Genesis 16) and cycles of stories (Abraham-Lot, Jacob-Esau-Laban, Joseph), brief (Penuel) and detailed (Genesis 24) narratives, the rough-hewn (Genesis 16) and the gentle (Gen 37:35), the ancient (Jacob-Esau story, Hebron story) and the late (Gen 12:1ff; 15), of a religious and moral kind, the vivid and the colorful from far off times, and those of faded hue. E is not that much different, containing for example the moving story of the sacrifice of Isaac (Genesis 22) and a variant of the very ancient story of Jacob's wrestling match (comm. pp. 359ff). This variety shows that the stories of E, and still more of J, do not bear the stamp of a particular period, not to mention that of an individual, but that they were in essence taken over by the collectors as they found them.

Second, a study of the variant readings of J and E [Ed. – i.e., the differences between J and E] teaches us the same. On the one hand, the two are often in striking agreement. For example, in the Penuel story they both use a brief style, and in the Joseph story a much more detailed and amplified style. Just because the two sources are so similar, a later hand was able to join them together in such a way that it is often impossible for us to discern where they flow into each other. On the other hand, they frequently diverge. J often has the older version, but at times E does. So J's (Genesis 16) rough-hewn story of Hagar is older than E's tearful version (Genesis 21); and in the narrative of the birth of Jacob's children, J speaks without any embarrassment of the magical effect of the "love apples" (Gen 30:14), whereas E insists on the effectiveness of the divine favor (Gen 30:17). In the story of Dinah, J, who describes Jacob's forebodings at what his sons have done, judges more justly and more basically than E, where God himself has to protect the sons (comm. p. 373). In the Joseph story the Ishmaelites of J (Gen 37:25), displaced in a later

period, are older than the Midianites of E (Gen 37:28; comm. p. 409).
E's account of Jacob's last testament, in which Jacob expresses his
wish to be buried with his beloved wife (Gen 48:7), is gentler and
more tender than J's, where Jacob asks only to rest in his own grave
(Gen 47:29ff; comm. p. 471), and so on. On the other hand E does
not know the Philistines of whom J speaks (Gen 21:32, 34; 26; comm.
p. 304), and Jacob's act of deception (Genesis 27) by means of
goatskins in E is more naive than J's aroma from the clothes. There
are still echoes of the original notion of the stone at Bethel as the
house of God in E, but no longer in J (comm. p. 322). In the story of
the treaty at Gilead there suddenly appears a subsequent Israelite
coloring in J only, but not yet in E (Gen 31:52; comm. p. 352). In the
Joseph story, Reuben, who was displaced in the historical period, has
in J the place later occupied by the much better known Judah.
Likewise, linguistic usage in E, which avoids the name Yahweh in
Genesis, rests on an ancient recollection which, as shown above (see
chapter 4), is missing in J. Nevertheless, one cannot fail to see that
the continual avoidance of the name of Yahweh before the time of
Moses indicates theological reflection that is foreign to J's style.

These observations, which could easily be multiplied, show also
that there is no immediate literary relationship between J and E; nor
has J taken anything from E, or vice versa. The frequent verbal
agreement between the two sources is to be explained from a
tradition that has related roots. But what matters here is to
recognize, from the way in which the stories have come together in
these books, that it is not a question of unified works or of
compilations of unified works, but of collections which have not been
struck from one die. They did not appear ready made, but arose in
the course of a history. This insight is the fruit primarily of a careful
study of the style of J, because most of the material in Genesis comes
from it.

We distinguish three sources in J's primeval story, two of which,
originally independent, present strands running parallel. It seems
very clear that J contained two parallel family trees of the primeval
ancestors, a Cainite tree alongside a Sethite tree, of which Gen 5:29
is a fragment. A third source was used when they were joined
together. The story of Cain and Abel, which cannot possibly go back
to the primeval period (comm. pp. 2-3), comes from it. We can
likewise discern three hands in the Abraham stories. First, there was
a cycle of stories dealing with the fortunes of Abraham and Lot.

Other pieces were inserted into it from another source. These include the stories of Abraham in Egypt and Hagar's flight (Genesis 16). Finally, a third hand added single pieces, such as Abraham's intercession for Sodom (comm. pp. 159ff). The composition of the Jacob stories is even more complicated. Some cult stories were inserted in the cycle of Jacob, Esau and Laban; eventually stories about Jacob's individual sons were added.

Though we can have an overall view of this process, we are no longer in a position to distinguish individual hands. Whereas the single primeval stories hang loosely together, some of the Abraham and Jacob-Esau-Laban stories have been woven into a closer unity; and the Joseph story is even more tightly knit (comm. pp. 395ff). The stories about Joseph in Egypt and his brothers form a well articulated whole, but the passage about his agrarian policy (Gen 47:13ff), which breaks the continuity, shows clearly that several hands were at work. Likewise, it is perfectly obvious that the story of Tamar (Genesis 38), which does not deal with Joseph, and the "blessings of Jacob" (Genesis 49), which is not a story but a poem, were inserted later.

The conclusion of this survey is that J is neither itself a unified work, nor does it go back to older, self-contained unities, but is the final result of the work of several, even many, hands. We see something similar in E as well, though there are only faint traces of it in Genesis. The two Gerar stories, for example, (Genesis 20; 21:22ff), which belong together, are now separated from each other by the history of Ishmael (Gen 21:8ff; comm. p. 233); and one thread of the Beer-sheba story derives from Abraham (Gen 21:8ff), the other from Isaac (Gen 46:1-3).

The history of the literary collection therefore presents a variegated picture, and we can be certain that we are able to glimpse only a small part of it. In the ancient period there would have been a whole literature of such collections, of which only fragments have been preserved for us, just as the three synoptic gospels present only the remains of a large gospel literature. The P source offers a proof for the correctness of this view; it is often related to J (P, like J, has a primeval story), and occasionally is in agreement with E (the name "Paddan," and the designation of Laban as "the Aramaean"). In certain details it adds entirely new traditions (the note that Abraham migrated from Ur of the Chaldeans, the narrative of the purchase of the cave of Machpelah, and so on, comm. pp. 101, 261-262, 385, 492).

But the most important observation for the entire picture of the history of the collections is that prefaced to these reflections: *the whole process had already begun in the oral tradition*. Stories were already joined together when the first hands wrote them down. Others added new stories, and in this way the whole material snowballed. Thus our J and E sources grew side by side. "J" and "E"
▶ therefore were not individual writers, but schools of storytellers. It is relatively unimportant what the different hands contributed to the whole, because individually they differ very little and will never
▶ permit of certain identification.

The Collectors and their Material

These collectors therefore were not the masters of their material but its servants. We should think of them as people filled with awe at these fine old narratives and intent on passing them on to the best of their ability. Fidelity was their prime characteristic. They took over so much that was only half understood and far removed from their own experience, and they often preserved details peculiar to individual narratives; e.g., the narrative of the wooing of Rebekah does not mention the city of Haran by name, whereas other passages in J are familiar with it (Gen 27:43; 28:10; 29:4, comm. p. 255). But the collectors were far from being limited to passing on the material without any alteration. They thought the stories through. The uniform use of language in the collections is a clear indication that there was a remolding of the material. We can come to a clear understanding of the mentality of the collectors from the impression produced on us by the whole that they created, even though (as is to be expected) the underlying conception that they had in mind is somewhat unformulated (cf. especially the primeval history, comm. pp. 1, 162). Later additions and reworkings also shed light on details. In particular we can attribute the spiritualizing of the material to them, as has already been noted (see chapter 4).

We gain a further insight into their way of working when we compare Genesis with the traditions of other ancient peoples and recognize its lofty religious and moral superiority (comm. p. 9). We think of the collectors, therefore, as people, far superior to the ordinary folk, whose purpose it was to raise the folk to the ideals they themselves had in mind by means of a great collection of these stories. They altered these stories in many ways. They joined

together different traditions (comm. pp. 475, 488), smoothed
contradictions between them (comm. p. 368), omitted much ancient
material, slightly revised other material (Gen 8:7; comm. p. 64), often
added little "notes," elaborated on motifs for which they had a
particular liking, put together different traditions, fashioned a new
sort of history (comm. pp. 378-379, 330), and so on. The process of ◄
reworking and accommodating the stories, already long at work,
continued further under them. It is difficult and most often nearly
impossible to distinguish in detail which of such alterations belong to
oral tradition, which to the collectors, and which to a still later period.
*Much of the reworking discussed above certainly took place only in the
written tradition.* One is inclined in general to ascribe an internal
artistic reworking to oral tradition, and a more external reworking
(which merely adds or omits) to the collectors or redactors. However
nothing decisive rests on this distinction. What matters is to grasp
the internal bases of the reworking.

At this stage some longer passages may have been omitted or
truncated. In the Hebron story, for example, the assurance in Gen
18:10 shows clearly that a continuation is expected which tells of a
second visit of the three men to Abraham, but this is missing and may
well have been left out by a collector (comm. p. 199). On the other
hand, some longer passages were not added until at the time of
writing; e.g., those family trees which are not fragments of stories, but
are only surveys of ethnographical relationships (Gen 22:20ff; 25:1ff).
Likewise, a passage like Abraham's dialogue with God before Sodom
(Gen 18:23ff) is of a type that indicates a later origin (comm. pp.
203-204), and so on. Also, a long, very ancient poem (Genesis 49)
has been added later to the stories.

We cannot see the whole picture of the alterations which
resulted from the process of collection. But despite the fidelity of the
collectors in detail, we can imagine that the overall effect of the
stories has been altered markedly by gathering them into large works,
and by the many revisions. The bright coloring of the individual
stories may well have blurred in the process; the original points may
have receded into the background when they were joined with other
narratives (comm. p. 176). And the different moods of the individual
stories might have balanced each other out when they stood side by
side. Trickery, for example, is no longer felt to be amusing when it is
joined with serious history (Gen 12:20; comm. p. 173). The spirit of a
loftier religion has suppressed the lower. Hence many of the

stories give the impression of an ancient, colorful picture heavily painted over and darkened by a later hand. Finally, it should be stressed that the fidelity of the collectors is especially evident in Genesis. The revisions in the later stories, especially in those about Moses, where there was a much more immediate religious involvement, may have been of a more fundamental nature.

The Schools of J and E

The two schools of J and E are very close to each other, and their essential harmony shows that they must belong to the same period. In the material that they transmitted, the collectors would have taken particular pleasure in the latest, namely in that which was closest to their time and experience.

The differences between J and E consist first of all in their linguistic usage, the most important of which is that J uses Yahweh, but E uses Elohim before the time of Moses. Further, J calls the patriarch "Israel" after his return to Canaan, whereas E calls him "Jacob." J uses *šiphāh* for the maid, E *'āmāh*. J calls the grain sack *śaq*, E calls it *'amtahat*, etc. In this case one should not (as we often do elsewhere) consider such linguistic usage to be the mark of a single pen, but rather of a circle or region. We are not in a position in very many cases to distinguish between the two sources on the basis of vocabulary. The decisive criterion is that the variants of the two sources present unified narratives, each of which is different in content. In J, Jacob deceives Isaac by the aroma of Esau's clothes, in E by means of the skins, a difference which dominates a great part of the two stories (Genesis 27). In other cases, different narratives have certain features or words running through them, as J having Joseph sold by the Ishmaelites to an Egyptian who was married, and E having him sold by the Midianites to Potiphar, an official of Pharaoh (see chapter 3). Often criteria of this sort are not at all clear, in which case we can only conjecture about the sources. Where there are no such differences there is no distinguishing of sources.

We cannot find the hand of E at all in the primeval story, which E probably did not have. E probably began with the patriarch Abraham. E. Meyer points out that the table of the nations and the ethnographical lists are also missing in E, and conjectures that E "did not envisage a classification of the Israelites in a general history of the nations and the world, as is the case with J" (*Die Israeliten*, p.

238). Often, though not always, J's tradition has preserved an older form than E's. J has the liveliest and most picturesque narratives, while E has a series of moving and tearful stories, such as the sacrifice of Isaac (Genesis 22), Ishmael's expulsion (Gen 21:8ff), and Jacob's tenderness towards his grandchildren (Gen 48:10b). The two sources are strikingly different in their conception of God's revelation. Ancient theophanies are important for J (e.g., Genesis 16; 18; 19), but E prefers dreams (Gen 21:3) and the call of the angel from heaven (Gen 21:17) — the most invisible means of revelation. It is E, and not J, who gives expression to the concept of divine providence, turning sin to good, in the Joseph story (Gen 50:20). Hence one is justified in holding, as is the common opinion today, that J in general is older than E.   ◄

J puts Judah in Reuben's place in the Joseph story, and preserves a specifically Judah tradition in the Tamar story. J also has much to narrate about Abraham who, so it seems, made his earliest settlement in the Negev (to the south of Judah) and his later one in Hebron. Hence, with many moderns, one can locate this collection in Judah. It is usually accepted that E, in contrast to J, originated in north Israel. Indeed, this source does have rather a lot to say about northern Israelite places, though it also speaks of Beer-sheba (Gen 21:32; 46:1). Furthermore, there is one passage in the Joseph story where E, in passing, presupposes the kingdom of Joseph (Gen 37:8), and that, too, likely reflects its tradition. One could mention other examples, but there can be no talk of any deliberate political stance in either of the collections favoring the northern or southern kingdoms; they are too faithful to their sources for that.

It is scarcely possible to derive any further characteristics of the collectors from Genesis. It would of course be easy to paint a colorful picture of J and E if one took the liberty of attributing to them everything that is found in their books. But this is precluded by the fact that they were collectors.   ◄

The Age of J and E

The question of the age of J and E is extremely difficult. We, who are of the opinion that it is a matter here of the progressive committing to writing of ancient traditions, have to divide this question into a series of subsidiary questions: When did these stories arise? When did they become known in Israel? When did they acquire in essence their present form? When were they written down? It is not our task, then, to fix a determined number of years, but to look for a long process over a period of time. This is a not an easy task, however, because generally speaking the chronology of intellectual processes is very difficult to fix. In addition (and this is an obstacle in other such Old Testament problems), we know too little of ancient Israel to propose anything certain. Moreover, other attributions of dates to Old Testament writings, in so far as they are the result of the study of the history of religion only, are not all as certain as is often thought. Here, too, our critical studies, if they are to remain sound, will have to take a good step backwards.

Many stories have their origin in a period that predates historical Israel. Israel must have already possessed the basic material of many stories about Abraham, Isaac and Jacob before its immigration. The family tree of the twelve sons of Jacob, which does not coincide with the localities of the tribes known to us, must reflect an older situation. Moreover, the concise style of the stories is very old. By contrast, the narratives about the "judges" are composed in the amplified style. Other material flowed in after the immigration into Canaan. It was then that the Babylonian stories of the origins were received through Canaanite hands. The material of the Joseph narratives, mostly from Egypt, was a further addition. Those stories, reworkings, and little "notes" which presuppose possession of the land and knowledge of Canaanite places, clearly come from the Canaanite period. The latest of the real "stories" deals with the regression of Reuben (Gen 49:3-4), the origin of the descendants of Judah (Genesis 38), and the surprise attack at Shechem (Genesis 34) – that is with events from the more ancient "period of the judges." No stories about the ancestors deriving from the later "period of the judges" are preserved, but rather, stories about the leaders of the tribes (see chapter 2), and no new stories about the ancestors would have been formed at this period. The age of the formation of the patriarchal stories thus closed at that time, about 1200 BCE [H. Gressmann puts the period when the great majority of the individual narratives were formed at 1300-1100, *ZAW* 30 (1910):34].

Other considerations prove that this determination is correct: an appendage to the story of the garden presupposes that "Ashur" lies west of the Tigris (Gen 2:14); this comes from a period when the Assyrian capitals of the east did not yet exist, and so before 1300. The reports at hand to P still preserve recollections of the pre-Israelite hegemony of the Hittites over Canaan (comm. p. 273). The derivation of Canaan from Ham is a lasting echo of the time when Canaan was a province of the kingdom of Egypt. On the other hand, there is no sign in the patriarchal story of the sanctuary in Jerusalem, so famous in the period of the monarchy—its foundation is set by the cult story in the time of David (2 Samuel 24). The long wars with the Philistines, the kingdom of Saul, the conflict of Saul with David, the unified kingdom under David and Solomon, the division of the kingdom and the war between the two, none of these have produced any aftereffects in the stories. Thus no new patriarchal stories could have arisen in this period. Signs of the later history appear only in the selection; the stories of the two leading tribes of Joseph and Judah are given preference among the tribal stories.

The period of the reworking of the stories follows that of their formation, covering in essence the older period of the monarchy. At that time when Israel, splintered into different tribes and regions, had been reunited into a unified people, the different traditions would have come together to form a common story of the people. The great upsurge which Israel experienced under the first kings would have given it the internal dynamism to take hold of the more ancient or appropriated narratives, to relate them to itself and, in part, to localize them in Canaan. The Jacob-Esau story (Genesis 27) was at that time applied to Israel and Edom. Israel had in the meantime subjugated Edom under David, and Judah held it as its own until about 840. Meanwhile Ephraim had overtaken Manasseh (Gen 48:13ff), perhaps at the beginning of the monarchy. There is an allusion to the kingdom of Joseph in the Joseph story (Gen 37:8; E), which found its way into the story only later. The horrible wars with the Aramaeans, which began about 900, are not evident in the Jacob-Laban story, which mentions only border skirmishes. The city of Ashur, occupied until 1300, is not mentioned in the table of the nations; but Nineveh, occupied since about 1000, is mentioned (Gen 10:11).

We can presume then that, as regards the narrative details, the stories have been essentially as we read them today since about 900. The only reference to political events after about 900 is the allusion to Edom's defection (about 840), and this is clearly an appendage to the story (Gen 27:40b). Nothing else that has been alleged by others proves anything. For example, it does not follow from the mention of

the Assyrian cities (Gen 10:11-12) that this information belongs to
the Assyrian period; Assyria had been long known to Israel. Nor can
any conclusion be drawn from the mention of Calah. The city was
▶ rebuilt in 870, but had been occupied since about 1300. [Ed. — We
now know that Calah was already occupied during the reign of
Hammurapi, at least 400 years earlier than Gunkel's date. Ashur was
already occupied when Shamshi-Adad I took it over in the 18th
century, BCE. It was the capital from the 14th century to the 9th,
when Calah became the capital. Nineveh, which was occupied at
least intermittently since prehistoric times, was also occupied during
Shamshi-Adad's time, and probably continually thereafter until its
destruction in 612 BCE. It became the capital in the early 7th
century. Discoveries not known to Gunkel have thus vitiated much
of the discussions of this and the preceding paragraphs regarding
Assyrian cities.] According to P. A. de Lagarde (*Mitteilungen*, III, pp.
226ff), W. Spiegelberg (*Aufenthalt Israels in Ägypten*, p. 26) and
others, the Egyptian names in Genesis 41 should lead us to the
seventh century; but there is no certain support for this as the names,
very common in that period, are also known in an older period (cf.
comm. on Gen 41:45).

Even if no new political allusions have intruded into the stories
since about 900, and the stories have retained their essential lines,
▶ they have nevertheless undergone many internal alterations. We
must therefore allow a much longer time for the religious and moral
adaptations to have taken place (these have been discussed above).
This period goes back beyond the time when the collection was made,
and concludes with the making of it.

The Writing Down of the Stories

When were the stories put into writing? This question is
particularly difficult because we have only internal grounds on which
to make a decision and we can only establish the grounds after fixing
the sources. Unfortunately we are moving in a circle, as we are with
many other of our chronological estimates, and there is no prospect
of our ever coming out of it. Scholars should reflect, both here and
elsewhere, before proposing all too confident solutions. Further, one
should note that the collections did not appear suddenly and ready
made, but are the result of a long process lasting decades or even
centuries. The real question in establishing the sources is, how do

the two of them stand in regard to "written prophecy?" There are, to be sure, in Genesis a number of points of contact with it, but the view of many moderns, that this contact must go back to the influence of the writing prophets, is in many cases very questionable; we do not know the religion of Israel well enough to be able to assert that certain ideas or attitudes first entered the world through those particular prophets whose writings we have, e.g., Amos. The seriousness with which the flood story speaks of sinfulness, and the glorification of the faith of Abraham, are not specifically "prophetic." The collectors' aversion to the *maṣṣēbōt*, which goes beyond J and is ◄ still present in E (Gen 28:22, and elsewhere), to the "golden calf," which the story in E regards as sinful (Exodus 32), and to the teraphim, of which the Jacob-Laban story makes fun so wittily (Gen 31:30ff) — none of these needs rest on the influence of the "prophets." These very attitudes could have existed in Israel long before the "prophets." Indeed, we must assume them in order to be able to understand the rise of the "prophets." To be sure, E calls Abraham a *nābî'* (Gen 20:7), and so is living at a time when prophet and man of God were the same. But the position of the *nᵉbî'îm* had blossomed long before Amos; and Hosea, too, calls Moses a "prophet." Nothing therefore prevents us from maintaining that J and E are in essence "pre-prophetic."

A number of considerations favor this. Written prophecy is distinguished by its foretelling of the destruction of Israel, by polemic against foreign gods and the holy places of Israel, and by the rejection of sacrifices and religious practices. It is these that characterize the "prophets" and they are not found in the stories of J and E. J has no thought at all in Genesis for gods other than Yahweh, and Jacob's rejection of foreign gods in view of Yahweh's action (Gen 35:4; E) does not sound "prophetic." Certainly in Genesis there is no talk of a polemic against foreign gods. Moreover, the founding of a number of altars and sanctuaries by the patriarchs has a very different ring from the passionate attack of the prophets against worship at these very places!

While these collections contain nothing specifically prophetic, they have nevertheless very much which must have been highly offensive to the prophets. In particular, they take a friendly attitude to the holy places which the prophets attacked so bitterly. They are at ease in the face of the old religion and morality, and this is in direct opposition to the fearful accusations of the prophets. We know from the prophetic revision of the historical books the attitude which the genuine disciples of the prophets took towards ancient tradition; they would certainly not have fostered the popular story that contained so much pagan material, but rather, would have extirpated it! One is left, then, with the conclusion that the collections in essence preceded the great period of written prophecy, and that the contacts with the spirit of this movement in J and E show how the prophetic ideas for a large part were in circulation long before Amos.

This follows further from two other considerations. First, the story of Abraham's departure (Genesis 12), which glorifies his faith, presupposes a state of prosperity and well being whose end was in no way expected. This certainly had its origin in a period before the Assyrian threat. Second, passages which, from the point of view of the history of the transmission of stories, are quite late, such as Genesis 15 or the story of the birth of Jacob's sons, nevertheless have very ancient religious motifs (comm. pp. 183-184, 330).

This, however, does not exclude some of the latest passages in the collections from being "prophetic" in the proper sense. Such is the case with Abraham's dialogue with God before Sodom. The content deals with a theological problem, the form is an invitation to prophetic "litigation" with God, and the prophetic threat of Israel's destruction is in the background (comm. pp. 204-205). Joshua's farewell speech (Joshua 24), with its frank mistrust of Israel's fidelity, is also in form an imitation of the prophetic sermon. There is still more of the same in subsequent books, particularly in E, but in Genesis there is but the one example (Gen 18:23ff).

Accordingly, we can set both collections as wholes in the period before the rise of prophecy, J somewhere in the 9th century, and E somewhere in the first half of the 8th; one must stress, however, that such precision with dates always remains very uncertain.

Both collections were united later by a redactor (R^{JE}) whom, following Wellhausen, we call the "Jehovist." This took place before the later book of stories of P was added. We can set this collector somewhere in the latter period of the state of Judah. R^{JE} proceeded with extraordinary care in Genesis and expended a considerable amount of ingenuity to preserve both sources as far as possible and to bring them into an appropriate unity, even though forced by the situation to omit much that was incompatible with the account received. In general, J (the more extensive source) was the basis of the Abraham story. The redactor rarely comes forward with an original contribution in Genesis. We can recognize this pen with certainty in a few brief additions which are directed at uniting variants of J and E, but they are relatively rare and most concern minor details (Gen 16:9-10; 28:21b; further, in 31:49ff; 39:1; 41:50; 45:19; 46:1; 50:11, and several in Genesis 34).

There are further additions, for the most part not very extensive, that we should set in this period, and could probably trace back to this redactor or contemporaries. Some of them paint the fine lines of the original text more heavily (Gen 18:17-19; 20:18; 22:15-18). Others are spiritual elaborations of secular stories (Gen 13:14-17; 32:10-18). Most are divine discourses (Gen 13:14-17; 16:9, 10; 18:17-19; 22:15-18; 26:3b-5, 24, 25a; 28:14; 32:10-13; 46:3abii; 50:24iii). These discourses are the latest additions. They present ideas rather than stories and are characterized by a solemn promise: Israel is to be a powerful and great people and possess "all these lands." This is the occasion for enumerating the peoples which Israel is to overcome (Gen 15:19-21; 10:16-18). These additions come from periods when great world movements threatened Israel's existence, and faith clung to these promises; thus probably from the Chaldaean period. Here and there "deuteronomistic" language also appears (i.e., a language that belongs to the period of "Deuteronomy," the law of the kingdom under Josiah, 623; e.g., Gen 18:17-19; 26:3b-5).

6
THE PRIESTLY CODE
AND THE FINAL REDACTION

The Source P and its Characteristics

This source is so different from the other sources in its language and spirit that it can be peeled off almost to the last word. Like the older collections J and E, it covers more than Genesis. Rather, the primeval story and the patriarchal stories are but a brief preparation for the main issue, the giving of the law by Moses. The priestly code is of special importance for us because an earlier age of Old Testament scholarship relied in essence on the data in it for its overall view. It is J. Wellhausen's undying service (*Prolegomena*, 6th ed., pp. 293ff) that he recognized the peculiar character of this source, which had to that time generally been regarded as the oldest, and thereby demonstrated the error of the earlier overall view; he thus prepared the way for a vital, genuinely historical understanding of the history of the religion of Israel.

P's style is unique. It is notably prolix and charged with legal clarity and completeness. It consistently employs the same expressions, formulas, precise definitions and monotonous phrases. Its schemata is logically worked through and has no padding. There are also family trees and headings to each chapter. The tone is that of prosaic scholarship, often indeed that of a legal document (e.g., Gen 11:11; 23:17, 18), but at times not without a certain solemn dignity (particularly in Genesis 1, but also elsewhere; e.g., the scene in Gen 47:7-11). One must read the whole source through at a stretch to experience the sobriety and monotony of this remarkable book. The author was obviously painfully precise and exemplary in love of order, but (like many scholars) lacked a sense of poetry.

The Material in P

The choice of material in general and in detail is very significant. Of the longer stories, P has only the creation and flood narratives, God's revelation to Abraham (Genesis 17) and the purchase of the cave of Machpelah (Genesis 23). The rest consists only of notes and family trees. P was capable of using only single remarks from most of the narratives. One only has to compare the colorful and poetic ancient stories with the sparse data that P takes from them to see that this author did not want to narrate in poetic style, as the ancients did, but to establish facts. Accordingly, P did not make use of many individual details which the ancient stories contained, but just took a few facts from them. The moods of the stories were abandoned, and the personal life of the patriarchs are not seen. These once concrete figures faded in P's hands. In the ancient period many of the stories took place at particular places and thereby acquired life and color. But P knows only two locales, the cave of Machpelah where the patriarchs lived and lie buried (Genesis 23), and Bethel, where God revealed himself to Jacob (Gen 35:6a, 11ff). All other places have been omitted. On the other hand, P has a predilection for family trees which, as we have seen (see chapter 5), are the latest addition to the process of transmission of the stories, and by their nature neither concrete nor poetic. A very large part of P in Genesis is nothing other than genealogy (Genesis 5; 10; 11:10ff; 25:12ff; 36).

Even the narratives, which in P are prolix and detailed, show the same pallor. They are not real "stories." The narrative of the purchase of the cave of Machpelah could have been merely a note
►   for an older storyteller, but P has spun it out at length, without having the poetic ability to shape it into a "story" (comm. pp. 273ff). In the affairs of leaders and government that P has in place of the old stories, it is no longer a matter of narrative, but rather, of talk and negotiation (J. Wellhausen, *Prolegomena*, 6th ed., p. 338). Even the creation and flood narratives and the covenant with Abraham (Genesis 17) are a long way from the lively and colorful style of the ancient story. They lack concrete narrative material. P gives something else in place of this which is certainly a long way from the spirit of ancient story, namely formal and prolix legal prescriptions (Gen 1:28ff; 9:1ff; 17:9ff); as what follows of P will deal in detail only with the giving of the law by Moses. A further characteristic of P is an unmistakable feeling for schemata. P's love of order has

imprisoned the colorful stories of ancient times within a grim pattern in which they have lost their poetic aura entirely. One only has to read the family tree of Adam (Genesis 5) and of Shem (Gen 11:10ff). P has even confined the patriarchal story within a schema.

P added to the stories a detailed chronology which played an important role for that author, but which is utterly unsuited to their simplicity. Chronology by nature belongs to history, not to story. When historical narrative and story flourish side by side as genres, one distinguishes the two, however unconsciously. The mingling of the genres in P shows that by then this natural sense for story and historical narrative had been lost. It is not surprising, then, that P's chronology produced some amusing oddities when inserted into the ancient stories. Sarah was still a beautiful woman at sixty-five and the Egyptians planed to ensnare her. Ishmael, a lad of sixteen, was carried on his mother's shoulders (comm. pp. 169, 229).

Again, P divides world history into periods and imposes this schema on the whole of the material. Four periods are distinguished: from creation to Noah, from Noah to Abraham, from Abraham to Moses, and from Moses on. Each of these periods begins with a revelation from God. Twice God is mentioned by a new name. He is called Elohim at the creation, El-shaddai in the Abraham story, and Yahweh in the revelation to Moses. When the "covenant" is concluded, specific divine ordinaries are proclaimed: first that man, woman and animals are to eat plants only (Gen 1:29-30), then after the flood, that animals may be eaten, but no one is to kill a person (Gen 9:3ff), next that Abraham is to circumcise himself and his descendants (Gen 17:9ff), and finally the Mosaic law. Particular divine blessings and promises are added and a sign of the covenant is given. What we encounter here is the product of a mind that embraces the whole world, the beginning of world history in grand style, just as elsewhere in P we observe a truly scholarly bent. One has only to think of the precision in the structure of the process of creation in Genesis 1 and the definitions there. But this splendid world history uses story material which stands in remarkable contrast to it. The "signs of the covenant" are the rainbow, circumcision, the sabbath — a most extraordinary list! This conception of world history, which undertakes to compass the whole course of time, is far removed from that of ancient story, which originally stood by itself as a single narrative, and never rose to such all embracing concepts. For example, in J we hear nothing of the relationship of the religion of Abraham to that of his ancestors and clansmen. We also cannot pass over P's idea that Yahweh first revealed himself quite generally as "God," then more specifically as El-shaddai, and finally with his own proper name without commenting that it is very childish. The real history of religion begins not with the general so as to arrive at the concrete, but on the contrary with what is very concrete. Humans come to grasp the abstract only in a long, slow process.

P, God, Religion and Morality

It is significant for the religion of the author that the priestly source says almost nothing about the personal piety of the patriarchs. For this source only the objective element in religion is of importance. There is not a word, for example, about Abraham's obedience in faith. Indeed, P was not ashamed to report that Abraham laughed when God made the promise (Gen 17:17). The religion which P knew consisted of practical ordinances: it was important that the sabbath was celebrated, that circumcision was practiced, that certain things were eaten and others not. P was very punctilious in these matters, but did not narrate that the patriarchs offered sacrifices at this place or that. This is clearly intentional and was because by then these locales were regarded as pagan. Likewise, no distinction was made in the flood story between clean and unclean animals. P was convinced that legitimate worship and the distinction between clean and unclean came only with Moses. We hear in this the priest of Jerusalem speaking, whose theory it was that the worship of the sanctuary alone is valid and is the continuation of the worship of Moses. Israelite theocracy, to express basic priestly thought in modern terms, is the goal of the world. God created the world so that his statutes and commands may be fulfilled at the temple in Jerusalem.

P's theophanies characteristically lack concreteness. It is only said that God appeared, delivered an address, and went up again (e.g., Genesis 17); everything else is left out. P follows here the latest additions in JE which likewise contain such divine addresses without introductions. The priestly source clearly manifests a religious reserve at implicating the superterrestrial God in the affairs of the world. It is as though the theophanies were suspected of having a pagan origin, as when P expunged completely even the angels whom were vaguely felt to be derived from polytheistic thinking (comm. p.

111). At the same time one can recognize a positive interest here; it is the content of the divine revelation that is important, not the "how." This is the spirit of an orthodoxy that is indifferent to history. And it is no chance that P thought of these divine addresses as contracting a covenant; the original legal form obviously suggests it to the author. This connection of the priestly, the scholarly, and particularly the legal is in reality quite natural, though perhaps at first strange to us. The priesthood is the guardian of scholarship and particularly of law among many ancient peoples; and it was certainly so in Israel, where the priests from time immemorial were wont to arbitrate difficult matters. P's style was fashioned after the written contract, and this is quite clear in many places.

It is particularly significant that P had nothing more to say about the sacred symbols which were so important in the ancient religion, as the stories of the patriarchs show. One reads nothing of the memorial stones, the trees and groves, or the wells, where, according to the ancient stories, God appeared. P rejected all this material, obviously because it was regarded as pagan. It is here that the effect of the fearful polemic of the prophets comes to the fore. The same spirit, which in the "reform" of Josiah cauterized the ancient shrine at Bethel as pagan, eliminated from the ancient stories everything that recalled this hankering after paganism. The ideas of God in P are certainly loftier and more developed than those in the stories; nevertheless, it is on a level far inferior to the ancient religion, which knew nothing of the "churchiness" of Jerusalem, but was well aware of what piety is. The best side of P appears in the famous, and for that author very important, account of creation (comm. pp. 116ff). Here P's style, despite its rather sober definitions and classifications, has a solemn dignity; and the very supernatural idea of God, to which P gives classical expression here, and which differs so markedly from all other creation myths, particularly from the Babylonian, makes this chapter a milestone in the history of revelation.

The priestly source purified the morality of the patriarchs no less than their religion. P appears here as the last word in a development which we have already followed in J and E. The old patriarchal stories, the expression of ancient folk life, contained much that later people, if they wanted to be quite honest, really had to regard as sinful and disgraceful. However, the later generation believed that the fathers were to be regarded as the model of piety and virtue. And so it took great pains to eliminate at least the coarsest scandals.

P was very busy clearing stuff away—by simply leaving out what was scandalous (e.g., the dispute between the herdsmen of Abraham and Lot, Lot's self-interest, the expulsion of Ishmael, and Jacob's deceptions). On occasion P even dared to maintain the opposite of the tradition—Ishmael and Isaac together buried their father peacefully (Gen 25:9), as did Jacob and Esau (Gen 35:29). Sometimes another explanation is given of facts which cannot be done away with—Isaac's blessing of Jacob is explained from Esau's sinful mixed marriages (Gen 26:34ff; 28:1ff), and the crime against Joseph is shifted to the sons of Bilhah and Zilpah (Gen 37:2).

P and the Tradition

The conclusion from all this is that P handled the tradition quite arbitrarily. Ancient traditions were altered or left aside at the author's discretion; notes were spun out into complete stories, or notes were all that might be preserved of complete stories. Motifs from different stories were mingled; e.g., it was maintained that the blessing that Jacob received from Isaac was the blessing of Abraham, something of which the ancient storytellers had never thought (Gen 28:4, other examples pp. 262, 271, 385). A continuous, self-contained narrative was fashioned from the loosely associated stories of the ancient traditions, and this, too, is a sign of a very late period. In place of stories, P created sections with regular headings. This narrator therefore knew nothing of the fidelity of the ancients and would have been under the impression that one had to make hefty inroads to erect an edifice worthy of God. J and E were not really "writers," but only collectors, whereas P was a proper "writer." The former merely heaped the building stones loosely together, but P erected a unified building designed by the author. However, it would be a mistake to believe that P built in Genesis according to personal specifications. At any rate, the tradition was too strong for that. Rather, P only reworked the material, but pretty thoroughly at that. There are many details by which we can see that the course of events in P's source was followed when priestly interests were not at stake (comm. p. 151-152). One should not, then, for this reason reject a detail found in P alone, but reckon with the possibility that it may have been taken from an older source. But this source, at least in Genesis, was neither J nor E, though it was related to them (comm. pp. 101, 261-262, 385, 492).

The Era of P

Following on the above, the era of P is clear. It stands somewhere at the conclusion of the whole history of the transmission, certainly separated by a long time gap from J and E. The creative period of the story, from which the old collectors J and E had fashioned their works, must at that time have been exhausted if P could treat the stories with such a heavy hand to construct the history of the priestly source. A gigantic spiritual revolution must have taken place in the meantime, one which had created something entirely new in place of the ancient lore lodged in the stories. P is the book of a period which deliberately renounced the ancient traditions, and believed that it had to lay the foundations of religion in a way different from that of the fathers. And the new that came to prominence at that time is quite clear to us from P; it is the spirit of the learned priest who is speaking here. Furthermore, it is clear from the overall style of P's approach that we are not dealing with the work of an individual with a particular line of thought, but with a whole circle of whose convictions this is the spokesman. P's writing is nothing less than an official manifesto. It came from the priestly families of Jerusalem. Hence the distinguishing name "priestly codex." Since J. Wellhausen, we know the era to which this spirit belongs. It is the period after the great catastrophe of the people and state of Judah. The people, deeply affected by the vast and horrible calamity that had struck it, realized that its fathers had sinned and that a great religious renewal was necessary. It is only in this context that we can understand P's formidable lack of piety with regard to the holiest traditions of the people.

We know well that it was the priesthood alone which, at that time, when all other authority had been ruined by mismanagement or had perished, still remained standing and held the people together. The community of Judah stayed under the domination of the priesthood after the restoration. It is to this period that the characteristic historically developed scholarship of P belongs. The earlier age had outstanding tellers of stories, but had produced no scholarly writers of history. During the exile Jewish history writing lost its naive simplicity. Under the powerful influence of a superior Babylonian civilization, Judaism too acquired an awareness for precision with numbers and measures. It became accustomed to be careful with statistical details. People copied down family trees, ransacked archives for reliable information, established chronologies and, in imitation of the Babylonian model, applied themselves to world history. This same appreciation of precise chronology is found also in Ezekiel, Haggai and Zechariah. This same historical scholarship, and particularly the family trees, is likewise in evidence also in Ezra, Nehemiah and Chronicles. The numbering of the months, found in P, also appeared in Judaism at this time. The progress which this scholarly mentality presents, in contrast to the naïveté of the earlier period, is unmistakable, even though the results of this scholarship are often unappealing to us. Large scale initial historical reconstructions, such as P offers, deal mostly with mythical or popular material and so are inadequate by our standards. But this is normal with the beginnings of "world history." One should compare P with Berossus in this respect.

The emphasis in P on the sabbath, circumcision, and the prohibition against shedding blood is also understandable for that period. Because everything rested on the free choice of the individual, religious commands which obliged the individual were stressed during that time. Indeed, one can say that the piety of the patriarchs, who are always presented as gērîm (aliens), and who have to get on without sacrifice and cult, is a mirror of the piety of the Babylonian exile, when in a foreign land one had no temple or sacrifice. Further, P's religious condemnation of mixed marriages, particularly with Canaanite women, whereby one forfeited the sharing in the blessing of Abraham (Gen 28:1-9), and the zeal with which family trees were collected, also point to this period when Judaism, scattered at large among the pagans, was striving for nothing more zealously than to keep its blood and religion pure.

But more certain still than these proofs that we take from Genesis are others which come from the legal passages in the books that follow. Ultimately, the argument is confirmed by the late origin of the language of P (J. Wellhausen, *Prolegomena*, 6th ed., pp. 385ff). P's date in the exilic period is one of the most assured results of source criticism.

The century in which P was written can remain a matter of indifference to us at this stage. However, one can say this much, that in the opinion of very many scholars, P is the law book of Ezra to which the community of 444 was obliged, and in the composition of which Ezra also had some part. We could thus probably set the composition of the book sometime between 500 and 444. P, too, was not the result of a single act of composition, a matter that scarcely comes into consideration in the case of Genesis.

The Final Redactor

The final redactor who joined together the older work JE and P (R^{JEP}) belongs therefore to the period after Ezra, and certainly before the schism of the "Samaritan" community which took the ◄ Pentateuch with it. That it was necessary to join together the old and the late collections shows us that the ancient stories had been buried too deeply in the heart for the new spirit to be able to expunge them. Mighty historical storms had in the meantime desecrated these holy places. The whole of the past was seen as sin; yet the ancient stories that glorified these places and mirrored that ancient period so innocently did not admit of destruction. P's attempt to stamp out what was ancient foundered, and a reverent and pious hand created a synthesis of JE and P. This last collection was done with extraordinary fidelity, particularly for P. Its author did not want to drop a single granule of P on the ground. We should not resent this preference for P over JE, for P was henceforth the complete master of Judaism. The redactor has used P's reckoning of time as the frame of the narratives of J and E. There is very little in Genesis that we can derive from a redactorial hand with any certainty: a few harmonizing glosses or fillings like Gen 10:24; 15:7, 8, 15; 27:46, as well as Gen 35:13, 14, some retouching in Gen 6:7; 7:7, 22, 23 and again in Gen 7:3a, 8, 9, as well as the distinguishing of Abram and Abraham, Sarai and Sarah (which is also in J and E), and so on.

This closes in general the work of the redactors on Genesis. But some editing of details of the text continued for a long time. We see minor revisions in Genesis 34 and in the numbers in the family trees, where the Jewish, the Samaritan, and the Greek versions differ from each other. More extensive additions and revisions took place in | Genesis 36 and 46:8-27. The last great insertion was the narrative of Abraham's victory over the four kings, a "midrashic" legend from a very late period.

Genesis is the confluence of many sources. It has remained in the form just mentioned—a form by which the ancient stories exercised an incalculable influence on later generations. One may perhaps regret that there was no last poetic genius to shape a great poetic whole, a truly "national Israelite epic," out of the individual |

stories. Israel produced great religious reformers who created a comprehensive unity with a religious spirit out of the scattered traditions of its people. But it never gave birth to a Homer. On the other hand, that may well be a blessing for scholarship. It is precisely because such a great poetic whole was not produced, and the pieces remained in essence side by side and not fused together, that we are in a position to perceive the history of the whole process. For this reason the students of story must go about their study of Genesis very differently than hitherto, and theologians must learn that one cannot understand Genesis without the study of story and especially the analysis of story.

Genesis and Moses

Now just a brief word as to how Genesis acquired the unmerited honor of standing as a work of Moses. There was a tradition in Israel from time immemorial that the divine prescriptions about cult, law and morality, as proclaimed by priestly lips, came down from Moses. When these prescriptions, which originally circulated orally, were written out in smaller or larger works, it was natural that they went about under the name of Moses. Our present Pentateuch consists, besides collections of stories, of such books of laws from different periods and with a very different spirit. And so it was the obvious thing to put both, stories and laws, together in one book, because the stories from the exodus on were mainly concerned with Moses. And so Genesis became the first part of a work of which the later parts spoke mainly of Moses, and which contained a variety of laws which would derive from him. But internally Genesis has nothing to do with Moses; the fiery spirit of this powerful, angry giant, which Moses must have been according to the tradition, and the spirit of these narratives, where there is so much that is humorous and gentle, are separated from each other by an enormous cleft. No one who reads Genesis without prejudice would ever imagine that Moses could possibly have been its author.

The biblical canon divides the whole work of the "Torah," the "Pentateuch," into five books; the Rabbis call the first of these by its first word, $b^e r\bar{e}'\check{s}\hat{\imath}t$, i.e., "in the beginning"; the Greek translation, known as the Septuagint, calls it "Genesis," i.e., the creation of the world, after the first narrative.

Conclusion

When in conclusion we survey the whole history set out in this book, we come to realize that it can almost be called a compendium of the complete history of the religion of Israel. And it is just because of this internal variety that Genesis makes such a solemn impression. Only the greatest creations of the human spirit bear comparison with it, such as the great cathedrals in whose form and adornment the spirit of many generations expresses itself, or states which have grown slowly in the centuries, or perhaps "Faust," the expression of a quite overpowering human experience. None of these tremendous creations are unities in themselves because they are more than the products of an hour. Nevertheless we do sense an inner unity in them which gives cohesion to their variety; it is the same people that itself built the cathedral and that supports the state. The devout observer who has arrived at this final stage cannot be denied to perceive this unity in the diversity of Israel's religious history as the guiding hand of God, who at one time spoke to children as children and then to adults as adults.

HERMANN GUNKEL
BIOGRAPHICAL DATA

1862   Johannes Heinrich Hermann Gunkel was born on May 25, 1862 in Springe, south of Hannover, the son of a pastor, Wilhelm August Philipp (1829-97). In the year of Hermann's birth, the family moved to Lüneburg where the father served as pastor of St. Nicolai until his death in 1897.

1881   Matriculation (*Reiferzeugnis*) in Lüneburg.

1881-85 Theological studies in Göttingen. In 1882-83, he attended the lectures of Adolf von Harnack and Bernhard Stade in Giessen.

1885-88 Gave private lessons in Lüneburg, Leipzig, and Göttingen to support himself.

1888   October 15 (originally set for July 21): Defense of theses for Licenziat in Göttingen. Dissertation: "Die Wirkungen des Heiligen Geistes." (Eng., *The Influence of the Holy Spirit*, trans. Roy A. Harrisville & Philip A. Quanbeck II, Philadelphia: Fortress, 1979).

        October 16: public lecture for *Habilitation*: "Die Eschatologie der judischen Apokalypsen."

        Gunkel was granted *venia legendi* for "Biblical Theology and Exegesis" in Göttingen for two years, the degree of *Habilitation*, and a stipendium for that period.

1890-94 Privatdozent for OT in Halle. Inaugural Lecture: "Die Eschatologische Erwartung des Judentums."

1894   It was during this period that Gunkel wrote his first
          important book, *Schöpfung und Chaos in Urzeit und
          Endzeit. Eine religionsgeschichtliche Untersuching über
          Gen 1 und Ap Joh 12*, 1895.

1895-1907 Prof. extra-ordinarius in Berlin (Gunkel was passed over
          twice for the chair of Ordinarius in Berlin, 1895 and 1899;
          in 1901 he almost became Ordinarius in Jena).

          "Das 4. Buch Ezra," in *Apokryphen 11* (ed. E. Kautzsch),
          1900, pp. 331-401.

          Genesis, 1901. The introduction to this 1st ed. of Genesis
          was published separately in Göttingen under the title, *Die
          Sagen der Genesis*, 1901, and was translated into English
          as *The Legends of Genesis* (trans. W. S. Carruth),
          Chicago: Open Court Press, 1901. It was reprinted as *The
          Legends of Genesis: The Biblical Saga and History*, (with an
          introduction by W.F. Albright) New York: Schocken
          Books, 1964; repr. 1984.

          The theology faculty of Berlin conferred a D. Theol.,
          honoris causa, on Gunkel for his *Genesis*.

          *Zum religionsgeschichtlichen Verständnis des Neuen
          Testaments* (FRLANT 1) 1903 (repr. 1910, 1930).

          Ausgewählte Psalmen, 1904 (4th ed., 1917).

          "1 Peter," in *Die Schriften des Neuen Testaments*, (ed.
          Johannes Weiss), 1906.

          "Die Israelitische Literatur," in *Die Kultur der Gegenwart*
          (ed. P. Hinneberg), 1/7, 1906, pp. 51-102 (repr. 1925; a
          3rd ed., Darmstadt: Wissenschaftliche Buchgesellschaft,
          1963).

During this period in Berlin, Gunkel was very active, especially during the vacation periods, in adult education. His courses for teachers in Jena were very popular. Such involvement at that time was very unusual for a university professor in Germany. The pioneers of NT form criticism, Rudolf Bultmann, Karl Ludwig Schmidt, and Martin Dibelius attended Gunkel's OT lectures in Berlin.

1907-20   Prof. Ordinarius in Giessen.

Genesis, 1910 (this 3rd ed., with the introduction and text fully revised, remained unaltered through the 9th ed., 1977).

Reden und Aufsätze, 1913.

Das Märchen im Alten Testament, 1917, 1921.

In 1911, the philosophy faculty of the University of Breslau conferred on Gunkel the D. Phil., and the theology faculty of Kristiania (Oslo) the D. Theol.

During the Berlin and Giessen periods, Gunkel acted as an editor of the series "Forschungen zur Religion und Literatur des Alten Testaments" (FRLANT) and of the 1st ed. of *Die Religion in Geschichte und Gegenwart.*

1920-27   Prof. Ordinarius in Halle.   This was the period of Gunkel's intensive work on the Psalms.

Die Psalmen übersetzt und erklärt, HKAT, 11/2, 1929.

Gunkel retired on October 1, 1927 because of ill health which had troubled him for many years.

1927-31   Further work on the Psalms. Editor-in-chief of the 2nd
           ed. of *Die Religion in Geschichte und Gegenwart*, 5 Vols.,
           to which he contributed 151 articles, some only short
           bibliographical or biographical notes, others very sub-
           stantial, e.g. Prophets, Psalms, History writing in OT,
           Sagen und Legenden.

1931   At Christmas, Gunkel handed over to his former student
           and collaborator, Joachim Begrich, his manuscript of the
           Einleitung in die Psalmen, which Begrich saw through the
           press in 1933.

1932   Gunkel died on March 11, 1932.

A bibliography of Gunkel's writings up to 1922 may be found in the
Festschrift presented to him on the occasion of his 60th birthday in
1922, EUXARIΣTHRION (FRLANT, NF 19, 1 & 2) 1923, pp.
214-225. For titles since 1922, see W. Klatt, *Hermann Gunkel*
(FRLANT 100), 1969, pp. 272-274.

Only the more important titles have been cited above.

In addition to those works mentioned at the beginning of the
discussion below on Gunkel's contributions to scholarship, the
following may be consulted for further information: W. Baumgartner,
"Zum 100. Geburtstag von Hermann Gunkel" VTSup 9 (1963),
reprinted in the 6th. ed. of Gunkel's *Genesis*, 1964, pp. CV-CXXII,
with literature cited; W. Klatt, *Hermann Gunkel* FRLANT 100,
Göttingen: Vandenhoeck & Ruprecht, 1969; F. Bovon, "Hermann
Gunkel, Historien de la Religion et Exégète des Genres Litteraires,"
and G. Rouiller, "L'Interprétation de Genèse 22, 1-19, par Hermann
Gunkel," in F. Bovon & G. Rouillet, edd., *Exegesis: Problèmes de
méthode et exercises de lecture (Genèse 22 et Luc 15)*, Neuchatel-Paris:
Delachaux & Niestle, 1975, pp. 86-97, 98-101; H. Rollmann, "Zwei
Briefe Hermann Gunkels an Adolf Jülicher zur religions-
geschichtlichen und formgeschichtlichen Methode", *ZTK* 78
(1981):276-288; R. Smend, *Deutscher Alttestmentler in drei
Jahrhunderten*, Göttingen: Vandenhoeck & Ruprecht, 1989, pp.
160-172.

HERMANN GUNKEL
Contributions to Biblical Scholarship

by John Scullion, S.J.

Hermann Gunkel was one of those influential and learned Old Testament scholars of the 19th and early 20th centuries who made a lasting contribution to biblical scholarship. His contributions continued throughout his academic life, from his early works as a Privatdozent in Halle, to his final work as Professor and Professor Emeritus in the same city until his death in 1932. They may be gathered under the following headings:

1. He affirmed the obligation of OT scholars to familiarize themselves with the history, culture, and literature of the ANE, and himself led the way: *Schöpfung und Chaos*, 1895.

2. He was a pioneer in the study of literary forms and oral tradition in the context of the OT: *Genesis*, 1901; 1910 (see also under 3).

3. He insisted that the study of the history of Israelite literature must be the study of the history of literary forms in Israel: "Die israelitische Literatur," 1906; *Das Märchen im Alten Testament*, 1917; "Literaturgeschichte," *RGG* III, 1929; "Sagen und Legende," *RGG* V, 1903.

4. He proposed a Religionsgeschichte that belonged entirely to the area of theology: *Zum Religionsverständnis des N.T.*, 1903.

5. He brought order into the study of the Psalms: *Ausgewählte Psalmen*, 1904; *Die Psalmen übersetzt und erklärt*, 1929; *Einleitung in die Psalmen*, 1933.

These contributions, at least in their broad outlines, are now standard tools of OT exegesis, whatever the modifications and corrections that have been brought to them in the meantime; cf. John H. Hayes, *An Introduction to Old Testament Study*, Nashville-London: Abingdon-SCM Press, 1979, pp.121-154, 254-260, 280-305; P. Gibert, *Une théorie de la légende: Hermann Gunkel et les légendes de la Bible*, Paris: Flammarion, 1979; S.M. Warner, "Primitive Saga Men," *VT* 29 (1979):325-335 (an inadequate critique of Gunkel's and Olrik's work); J. Van Seters, *Abraham in History and Tradition*, New Haven-London: Yale Univ. Press, 1975, pp.131-134, and index under Gunkel, p.316; *In Search of History*, New Haven-London: Yale Univ. Press, 1983, p.38, and index under Gunkel. C. Westermann builds on, modifies, and corrects Gunkel throughout the three volumes of his *Genesis*, Minneapolis-London: Augsburg Publishing House S.P.C.K., 1984-85-86.

The Bible and the ANE

At the beginning of *Schöpfung und Chaos* (*SuC*), Gunkel noted that up to his time there had been little interest in the origin and transmission of the narratives in Genesis. Was Genesis 1 of Babylonian origin? and if so, to what extent? Gunkel undertook a systematic study of the relationship between Genesis 1 and the Babylonian creation story. He pointed out that much of the material in Genesis 1 was not the creation of writers in Israel, but came from elsewhere; therefore, it had a history on its way into the text of Genesis.

The Primeval Monster

Gunkel discussed in detail all biblical references, outside Genesis, to the primeval dragon, Rahab, Leviathan, and the dragon in the sea as well as to the tradition of the primeval sea (*SuC*, pp. 29-114). He argued that the theme of the primeval dragon was well known. He also discussed a series of poetic passages in the OT which speak of the sea, but without any mention of mythological parallels. Gunkel perceived the following religio-historical sequence:
    1) the original Marduk myth
    2) a poetic recension of the Yahweh myth
    3) Genesis 1

In connection with Genesis 1, he concluded that the Babylonian myth came to Israel where it lost much of its mythological character and almost all polytheism and became almost fully Judaized (p.120). Genesis 1 should be regarded as a reworking of ancient Israelite tradition. The Babylonian material was taken over by Israel at an early period. The material about *tohû wābohû*, creation, and so on must have been at hand to the prophets, and so existing in Israel in pre-exilic times, i.e. in the Assyrian period (pp.121-170). Gunkel was very aware of the Canaanite background and what we might call the Canaanite "filter." With typical insight he observed that "we might suspect that a good number of the Genesis stories, namely those which belonged originally to certain sacred places, are of Canaanite origin" (pp.151-52). He maintained that the creation myth was taken over at a very early period and that the creation stories were very old (pp. 155, 160).

Revelation 12

Gunkel was convinced that the myth of Revelation 12 was of neither Christian, nor Greek, nor Jewish origin. Judaism had taken over preexistent material which the author of Revelation took over in his turn (pp.235-92). Revelation 11; 12; 13; 17 are four different recensions of a tradition about the same beast (pp. 337-41): 12:10,12, the hymn over the fall of the dragon, are due to the Jewish redactor. Gunkel concluded that the purport of the myth as used in Revelation was as follows:

> Just as a person, whose conduct and suffering determined the fate of his descendants, stood at the summit of human existence of old, so will the new humanity be inaugurated by a new figure who will bear his image. Just as the sin and death of the first Adam, the old man, was decisive for the earlier period, so will the uprightness and life of the new man the second Adam, be for the second.
>
> Just as the serpent seduced the first humans, so will it seduce the human race again before Christ returns.
>
> Paradise was the dwelling of the first couple; in the last time it will be humankind's dwelling again (4 Ezra 6:1; 7:53; 8:52). Then will the race share in the tree of life which it did not

taste in primeval time (Rev 7:17; 22:2, 14,19; 21:2; 1 Enoch 24-25; 4 Ezra 8:52).

Likewise, the exodus from Egypt, Israel's first liberation, and the appearance of the Messiah, the final liberator, are compared with each other. The plagues, which precede the end time, are conceived as analogous to the plagues of Egypt; the second liberator, Christ, *go'ēl 'aḥărôn*, is analogous to the first, Moses, *hārri'šôn*. Likewise the judgment of the flood and the world judgment at the end are parallel: "as in the days of Noah, so will the appearance of the son of man be" (Matt 24:37); the old world was destroyed by water, but the present will be preserved for a judgment by fire" (pp.367-69).

Gunkel brought his long study to a close thus:
> We have seen by means of the creation myth how Babylonian tradition made many fruitful contributions to Israel. Genesis 1 and Revelation 12 are typical of the way in which material was taken over and adapted. It is basically the same material that appears in the two, but in different forms. In the older period, it was a myth of primeval time that had come over to Israel from Babylon; in the later period, it is a prophecy about the end time. The attitude and the needs of humanity had altered in the meantime, in Babylon no less than in Israel (p.398).

Genealogy, Not Analogy

Gunkel was not looking for analogy in parallel ANE texts so much as for genealogy; i.e., he aimed at tracing the history of an idea, a symbol, or an image from Mesopotamia, or elsewhere, through early Israel to the biblical text.

Literary Forms, Oral Tradition, Genesis

Literary Influences

The introduction to the first edition of *Genesis* in 1901 covered seventy-one pages; the introduction to the 3rd ed. in 1910, ninety-four. The first edition carried scarcely a reference to literature in general or to literary critics in the field of *Germanistik* (the study of German language, literature, and history of literature). The third edition carries a number. Gunkel saw his own approach to folk story confirmed by Axel Olrik's influential essay, "Epic Laws of Folk Narrative" (Danish, 1908; German 1909; English in Alan Dundes, ed., *The Study of Folklore*, New Jersey [Englewood Cliffs]: Prentice-Hall, 1965, pp.129-141). Gunkel did not take over directly or consciously a method from *Germanistik*. He received stimulus from the Grimm brothers (Jakob, 1785-1863, Wilhelm, 1786-1859); he was in debt to Johann Wolfgang Goethe (1749-1832) and to Johann Gottfried Herder (1744-1803), especially to Herder's *Vom Geist der ebräischen Poesie*, 1782-83. They were the leading figures coming out of the *Sturm und Drang* movement of the second half of the 18th century which freed the German *Geist* from the confinement of French classicism (*Sturm und Drang*—the movement was at its height 1765-85—was the name of a play by Friedrich Maximilian Klinger, 1752-1831). But it was Gunkel alone who worked out his theory of the history of literature, literary forms, and story as applied to the Bible, though under the influence of Herder's "esthetic contemplation."

Sage and History

The introduction to all editions of *Genesis* stands under the title, *Die Sagen der Genesis*, and the first section carries the heading, "Die Genesis ist eine Sammlung von Sagen," ("Genesis is a collection of stories"). The German word *Sage* means folk story, popular story, or simply story, with no bias either way as to whether it narrates what really happened or not. It is not the equivalent of the English "saga," and to translate it by "saga" is very misleading. Gunkel puts great emphasis on *Sammlung*, "collection." The editors were collectors rather than redactors; they were more subject to the stories than were the stories to them, more servants of the material than its masters. The Yahwistic source, J, is a collection of collections. The collectors did, however, supply link passages. They received passages that had already been woven into a unity, or they supplied the unity themselves. They left other stories hanging loosely together.

Gunkel confronted the problem of *Sage*, story or folk story, in the Bible. "Story (*Sage*) is popular, poetic narrative, handed down from of old, dealing with people or events of the past. The word is

used here solely in this generally acknowledged meaning." He goes
on to ask "If . . . the Old Testament makes use of so many poetic
forms, why not of this?" He understood story as "the way of
transmission of those groups which are not familiar with writing;
history belongs to the scholarly occupations and presupposes the skill
of writing." History is only possible within a fixed and sophisticated
political structure. He distinguishes story (*Sage*) and history: 1) story
is in oral tradition, history is written down; 2) story deals with
personal, private, and family affairs, history with great political
events; 3) story derives from tradition worked over by imagination,
history from eyewitnesses, documents, and reports; 4) story moves in
the area of the incredible, history is the world we know well; 5) story
is poetic by nature, i.e., poetic prose, history is by nature normal
prose. For example: history narrates how and why David freed Israel
from the Philistines; story narrates how the boy David slew a
Philistine giant.

   Sage, or story, does not raise the question of belief or unbelief.
The question raised is that of a deeper understanding and a more
refined perception so as to decide whether the narrative handed
down is story or history. The story 1) is often in collision with genuine
historical tradition,   2) is at times intrinsically incredible, 3) intro-
duces the divinity in person, 4) is embellished history, not debased
history, 5) aims to entertain or engage the attention. The narrator of
the story believes what he is narrating. The *Sage* gradually moves
into the short story or novelette (Joseph story). It was Gunkel who
gained acceptance for the now accepted thesis that religion and
religious truth can be conveyed as adequately through story as
through history.

Types of Story

   Gunkel distinguished two types of stories in Genesis: 1) stories
about the origins of the world and the primal ancestors of the human
race, i.e. up to and including the story of Babel in Genesis 11; here
we are in primeval time, prehistory in the strict sense; the sphere of
interest is the whole world; 2) stories about the fathers of Israel and
their sons. Here we are within the framework of history; the sphere
of interest is the family, one family, with the notion that God's people
is to come from this family always in the background.

The divinity is the main actor in the primeval stories. But are these stories no more than faded myths? asks Gunkel. For Gunkel, "myths" are stories about the gods. But whatever of the mythical there is in primal Genesis, he insists, has come down in very faded colors. Israel did not tolerate unadulterated myth, at least in prose (mythical concessions *were* made to the poet, who was expected to subordinate the myth to the one God of all). Genesis had no pure myths of its own.

Many a story in Israel was an answer to a question asking the cause of something. These etiological stories were 1) geological: whence this desolate geological formation? (Genesis 19); 2) etymological: how did this place get its name? (Gen 11:9; 16:14; 22:14); 3) ethnological: whence the Ishmaelites? (Gen 16:12; 21:13); 4) cultic: why is this a holy place? (Gen 28:10-22).

Cycles of Stories

Gunkel reflected on the cycles of stories about Jacob-Esau-Laban and the traditions about Shechem; he saw in them echoes of the history of civilization, the experiences of peoples, or historical experience clothed in story. This led him to one of his most important reflections on the nature of *Sage*: we do not perceive ancient events clearly in the *Sagen*, but rather as it were through a mist. The story has spun its poetic web over the historical reminiscences and obscured its outlines; the process of transmission within the people has made its own medley of contributions; and so figures of entirely different origins have coalesced to form ancestors, and the historical and the imaginative have been woven into a single, unified web. The result is that the period in which the event took place cannot for the most part be determined from the story; often, not even the place is certain, and now and again not even the matter at issue. These stories obscure rather than reveal the events of the past; but only a barbarian would for that reason despise them. They are often more precious than straightforward prose accounts of what happened. For example, if we had an accurate historical account of Ishmael, we would remain more or less indifferent to it because Ishmael, in the biblical story, scarcely accomplished anything for the human race; but because poetic imagination depicted him as this "wild ass of a man" (Gen 16:12), he lives for ever.

Esthetic Appreciation

Gunkel was always sensitive to the esthetic side of the stories. He considered an esthetic appreciation of biblical narratives an essential element of exegesis. He saw no conflict between the esthetic aspect and serious scholarship (*Wissenschaft*). He wrote in the foreword to the first edition of Genesis that "a treatment of the Old Testament in which philology, archaeology, or 'criticism' alone predominate, is inadequate." And in the foreword to the third edition he asked, "How long will it be before Old Testament scholars finally perceive the great problems that the history of literature poses to them in the area of narrative, and when will the testament left by the great Herder be executed?"

According to Gunkel, and others, the stories of Genesis were already old when they were written down. Genesis is the setting down in writing of popular tradition. The story is the joint creation of the individual storyteller and the people. Reshaping took place unconsciously, at least in the early stages; one can only speak of conscious recasting in the latest formations. The narrator and the listener regarded the stories as "true" accounts. The OT narrators pass almost imperceptibly from stories to properly "historical" narratives and go on to mingle the fabulous with the historical. This follows from the very nature of stories which in all seriousness substantiate contemporary realities. The popular story is the individual, independent story. It is this that claims attention. As one moves from one emotion to another, one needs a pause. The skilled storyteller provides it and the alert collector or editor is sensitive to it. So we have, "Now after these things . . ." The narrative span is usually very short, ten to fourteen verses; e.g. Abraham and Sarah in Egypt (Gen 12:10-20), Hagar's flight (Gen 16:1-14), Jacob at Bethel (Gen 28:10-22). Gunkel comes back often to what he calls "the limited span of attention" (*geringe Aufnahmefähigkeit*) *of an ancient people, a presupposition with which few would agree today (cf. J.W. Rogerson, Myth in Old Testament Interpretation, BZAW 104, Berlin, 1974, pp. 57-66.)* But there is also the detailed narrative, like the wooing of Rebekah (Genesis 24). This increase in detail and expansion is, for Gunkel, a sign of later development. Gunkel goes into great detail in the third edition to show that these brief narratives accurately fit Olrik's ten epic laws. Action takes precedence over character. And the action is always tightly knit.

Gunkel was very sensitive to the narrative dexterity of the storyteller. To give but one example: in Genesis 18, three travelers stand in the heat of the day at the entrance to Abraham's tent; they are offered hospitality; they sit at table and engage in conversation; they turn the conversation into a promise of a son to Abraham and Sarah. They are "messengers of the Lord," and in v. 10 they are the Lord himself.

The material of the stories is so old that the origin of the story is ever beyond the gaze of the scholar and goes back to prehistoric times. Gunkel is right here. Furthermore, the material for the most part does not come from within Israel; he is right here in some cases. As far as we can discern, continues Gunkel, the overall picture of the transmission of the stories is broadly as follows: the primeval story is essentially Babylonian in origin; the patriarchal story is essentially of ancient Hebrew origin with some inserts from Israel's historical period; the Joseph story looks towards Egypt. Canaan mediated the primeval story to Israel; this we may endorse. But Canaan had no influence on the patriarchal story as a whole; this we may query. Gunkel says that Israel was too proud to have taken over ancestral figures from the Canaanites, and too clearly aware that it was not at home in Canaan and had no blood ties with that land.

The Religious Meaning of Story

One of Gunkel's chief aims was to grasp the religious meaning of the Old Testament by means of the *Sagen*. While he was grappling with this problem, he discovered that with a poetic genre when dealing with the *Sage*. How does this poetic genre come to terms with the divinity, with God? What does one conclude about the divinity from the stories in Genesis? The divinity is bound to the night at Penuel, "Let me go, for the day is breaking" (Gen 32:22). (Cf. "It faded on the crowing of the cock," "But even then the morning cock grew loud, and at the sound it shrunk in haste away," Hamlet, act 1, scenes 1 & 2). But it approaches in the heat of the day by the oaks of Mamre (Genesis 18). It appears as a smoking pot and flaming torch at the covenant with Abraham in Genesis 15, but without a sign at all at the spring on the way to Shur to comfort Hagar (Genesis 16). Its locale is the fertile land whence it addresses Cain (Genesis 4), but it reveals itself to Abraham on the steppes of distant Haran (Gen 12:1-3). It is involved in the minutest household affairs in the birth of the children of Bilhah and Rachel (Genesis 30), but dominates the whole world which it has formed in the account of the flood (Genesis 6-8). It scrutinizes the secrets of the heart in the case of Onan (Gen 38:10), but has to go down to the place itself to see what is going on at Babel (Gen 11:6) and Sodom (Gen 18:21). It appears in person to act and speak in the testing of Abraham (Genesis 22), but works in hidden ways in the Joseph story, holding in its hands the thread of what is happening. God is incomparably superior to the human person in Gen 24:50 where Laban says, "The thing comes from the Lord, we cannot speak to you bad or good," but God is concerned about human power which is becoming great in the Babel story (Gen 11:6). But always, and without exception in the recensions at hand to us, God is one. Yet it is impossible, concludes Gunkel, that one and the same divine figure is behind all this. The stories are subjugating foreign material to Israelite belief. However, we must be cautious. The religion of Genesis is not simply the religion of Israel, as Hugo Gressmann had correctly observed. One should not, for example, attribute the idea of God found in the Penuel story about the wrestling match to the oldest period of the historical Israel, but to pre- or extra-Israelite circles which contrived the narrative. Israel was continually accepting and reshaping. Genesis shows us how superior ideas struggled with inferior material and gradually reshaped it into story.

Patriarchs and History

As he looks back and surveys the history and religion of the patriarchs, Gunkel observes that when we maintain that figures like Abraham, Jacob and Isaac are real persons and not derivations from mythology or astrology, that does not mean that they are historical; they are no more so, he notes, than Brünnhilde or Siegfried must be historical, though their names, too, are personal names. For Gunkel, the most important of the patriarchs are figures of poetic imagination, and the "religion of Abraham" is really the religion of the storytellers which they ascribe to him. One may express serious reservations here.

Israelite Literature

Gunkel acknowledged without difficulty that there must always be a place in biblical scholarship for that literary criticism of the individual books of the OT which makes up a substantial part of the traditional introduction to the OT. But he insisted that this was only a part of the task incumbent on OT scholars. They must come to terms with Herder's suggestions and the development which they stimulated, and see the literature as an expression of the life of this ancient civilization.

The Essential Types (*Gattungen*)

Modern literary criticism is as much a history of the writer and his works as a confrontation with what has been written. We know who the author was, when and where the writing was done. We do not know the authors of most of the books of the OT or when they were written; but we do know that many of them are collections which have been edited, redacted, and interpreted (see above). Ancient Israelite society was not a writing society. The life of the people was lively and passionate. All high points in life were accompanied by song. Victory in battle exploded into "I will sing to the Lord, for he has triumphed gloriously" (Exod 15:1); there was the Hebrew riddle (Judg 14:18), the dirge over the individual (2 Sam 1:19), the simple "Praise the Lord" of the Psalms, the royal marriage song (Psalm 45), the magic words (Deut 21:1-9), the liturgical formula (Num 6:24ff), the chant when the ark was moved (Num 10:35), the song at the digging of the well (Num 21:17-18), the song of the choir before the gates of the temple (Ps 24:7ff). Many of these "two-liners" were brought together, expanded, and written down. These formulas are the basic types (*Gattungen*). They did not have their origin at the writer's desk, but in the life of the people. To understand them, it is necessary to understand the setting in life. This is all the more important as there were many such types in ancient civilization which we no longer possess and so are not immediately evident to us.

The history of Israelite literature, then, consists in separating out the types in these collections and asking how these simple, independent pieces originally arose. It must describe the history of the types. This is fundamental to the understanding of Gunkel's conception of the history of Israelite literature. His guiding principle was that it is impossible to grasp completely the content of a Hebrew text if one has not recognized its type and form. From his study of the biblical texts, Gunkel arrived at the following description of a literary type (*Gattung*): it must exhibit, 1) a common store of ideas and attitudes, 2) a clear and constant form of speech which expresses, 3) a setting in life from which alone the content and form can be understood ["Die israelitische Literatur," 109 (1925), p. 57; H. Rollmann, "Zwei Briefe Hermann Gunkels an Adolf Jülicher", *ZTK* 78 (1981):276-288, esp. p. 284].

Märchen, Mythos, and Sage

In the first edition of *Genesis*, Gunkel traced a direct path from *Mythos* (myth), which he regarded as primal, through *Märchen* (tale, fairy tale, folk tale), to *Sage* (story, folk story, popular story). In the third edition he had come to the conclusion that the *Märchen* was primal, and that *Mythos* and *Sage* had their origins from it. He was convinced that there was a rich *Märchen* or fairy tale tradition in Israel on which the biblical writers drew. In *Das Märchen im Alten Testament*, 1917, Gunkel classified and discussed the various sorts of folk tales: 1) tales of nature (fables, Judg 9:8-15); 2) tale motifs about animals (Num 22:21-30); 3) tales about tools and utensils (1 Kgs 4:1-7; 4:42-44; 6:1-7); 4) tales about spirits, demons and ghosts (Gen 32:23-32); 5) tales of giants (1 Sam 17:4ff.); 6) tales of magic (1 Kgs 4:4-5); 7) tales of people's "spirit" (Judg 16:4-16, Samson's strength in his hair; 1 Sam 10:10; 19:23, Saul; and we could add "life in the blood," Lev 17:11 and Deut 12:23); 8) tales of children (1 Samuel 1); 9) tales of young men and women (1 Samuel 17); 10) assorted tales about people (2 Samuel 12); 11) tales about particular professions—cobbler, smith, tailor—(Gen 4:20-22); 12) tale motifs in the primeval story; e.g., the serpent. There is an extraordinary variety of material in the folk tale. However, Hans-Jürgen Hermisson, in his article in *Enzyklopädie des Märchen*, 1, 1977, pp. 419-441, concludes that "a great number of motifs which Gunkel (1917) claimed to be *Märchen*-motifs are simply elements from the world picture current at the time, or from myths of the surrounding world." But there are *Märchen*-motifs in the Bible, e.g. the talking snake (Gen 3:1-7), Moses' staff changing from staff to serpent,

Balaam's speaking ass (Num 22:28-30), Elijah's mantle (2 Kgs 2:8), and Elisha's floating iron axe head (2 Kgs 6:3-7).

Märchen, Sage, and Yahweh

According to Gunkel, the *Märchen* acquired historical reminiscences in the process of transmission through history, and so was transformed into story and legend (*Sage, Legende*). The main bulk of *Märchen* material remained and was applied to historical figures. The *Märchen* was familiar with subordinate divine beings. But Israel's Yahweh would tolerate no divinity beside him. Hence, Yahweh or his messenger suppressed the lower deities in these narratives; e.g. Yahweh has taken the place of the god of the spring in the Hagar story (Genesis 16); according to Hos 12:4, Jacob wrestled with Yahweh's messenger, Gen 32:23-32; it was an angel of God, not the spirit of a dead person, as the pagan story told it. Gunkel noted that the whole tone of the folk tale was raised and its quality changed when Yahweh entered. The history of the Yahweh religion is, up to a point, the history of the struggle against the folk tale.

Gunkel finishes his treatment of the *Märchen* with a survey of the material according to form and content. The folk tale is highly imaginative and is characterized by a ready credulity and an extraordinary sensitivity to the real world. The primitive belief, reflected in the folk tale, confers something of human life on all nonhuman objects.

Legende (Legend)

The legend is a narrative about persons animated by what Gunkel calls a new spirit; the legend is a "spiritual" (*geistliche*) narrative; e.g. the stories of the rise of the monarchy and the succession (Samuel, Saul, David).

Prophets

It is characteristic of and proper to the prophet, wrote Gunkel, to reveal the thoughts of God; and it is easier to do this by means of verbal address than by writing. The prophet proclaimed. The prophets moved from being speakers and proclaimers to being writers, and that in a historical period whose broad lines are known to us. They spoke in short, sharp bursts; they took over and used a great variety of types of speech which they adapted to their own ends. Writers then took over these pronouncements and impressed on them their own style and personal touch. The poet who produced the book of Job was heir to a rich store of types of speech and hymns on which he stamped his own poetic genius.

Israelite Literature and the Institution

It was Gunkel's opinion that a catastrophe burst over the most ancient Israelite literature and all but destroyed it. This catastrophe was the foundation and institution of a religion and a people by Moses. From that time, the life of the people was determined by two factors, Israel and Canaan. The union of primal Israel and primal Canaan to form a new people is basic to an understanding of the religion and literature of historical Israel. Gunkel did not have a high opinion of the contributions of the priestly school(s) and the chronicler(s).

Gunkel's Religionsgeschichte

Gunkel's "school" of the history of religion was not part of the general "History of Religions" movement, but a movement belonging entirely to the area of theology. It was not "comparative religion." Prominent members of the so-called "circle" were, A. Eichorn (1856-1927), W. Wrede (1859-1906), W. Bousset (1865-1920), and H. Gressmann (1877-1927).

Gunkel's approach to the history of religion was determined by his general historical-theological outlook. His first axiom was that revolutionary and influential ideas in the history of the human race (and religious ideas are foremost among these) make their breakthrough only after a long process of struggle. They achieve clarification in outstanding personalities. But these personalities are not alone the decisive element; they are carried to the forefront by the anonymous historical movements behind them. According to Gunkel, this is true not only of persons who were prominent in their time, but also for lesser persons.

A second Gunkel axiom was that revelation is neither opposed to history nor outside the course of history, but takes place within the history of the human spirit; all manifestations of the spirit (*Geist*) in literature and religion are to be understood historically. Hence, Gunkel's formula, *Menschheitsgeschichte als Offenbarungsgeschichte*, the history of the human race as the history of revelation. He was convinced of the revelatory character of history.

Gunkel's *Religionsgeschichte* was really a continuation of his work in *Schöpfung und Chaos*. His point of departure was the book of the Revelation of John. Many, if not all, the images, symbols, and ideas there came from outside Israel. The seven torches (Rev 4:5), which are the seven spirits of God, reflect a submerged polytheism; in fact, Jewish angelology was nothing else than submerged polytheism. The seven angels go back to seven gods which go back to the seven planets. The twenty-four elders were originally the twenty-four Babylonian astral deities. The heavenly Jerusalem goes back to an original city of the gods which lay along the Milky Way. The locusts, the fierce horsemen, and the plagues all go back to mythological representations (the "Panbabylonianism" and astral speculations of H. Winckler and A. Jeremias were in the air in the first decade of the century).

Gunkel extended his approach to the whole of the NT, in particular to the persons of Jesus and Paul. For example: Judaism had constructed an image of the anointed one (Messiah) out of mythological elements. Early Christians were convinced that Jesus was the anointed; so the anointed construct was applied to Jesus. Primitive Christology was not just the result of the impression made by the historical Jesus, whose role was very subordinate. The main elements of Christology derived not from the historical Jesus, but were independent of him and had their origin elsewhere. The same is true of Paul. The question must be raised, Gunkel wrote, whether it is legitimate to derive from the once and for all experience of an individual (Paul's experience on the way to Damascus) a historical thing of such significance as Paul's Christology. No, said Gunkel; much of Paul's Christology derived from other sources. Gunkel did not think that Jesus or Paul as persons were all that influential and dominant in their time; he subordinated them both to his general historical-theological outlook. Nor did he always adequately distinguish what Jesus and Paul and the early Christian community inherited, and how they used their heritage; it was not just the automatic application of something ready-made, but often a thorough reworking of what had come to them. Theologians and historians of early Christianity have dealt adequately with Gunkel's confused and confusing presentation.

If revelation comes out of the study of the history of the human spirit, what is the special contribution of Jesus and Christianity? Gunkel answered: whatever the origin of the idea of the resurrection, what matters is the unique use that Christianity made of it. Christ in his resurrection brings life to light, and we experience it with him when we unite ourselves mystically with him. A mysticism and a theology of history seem to move on parallel planes.

The Psalms

Gunkel's commentary on the Psalms, covering over six hundred dense pages, appeared in 1929, four years before the Introduction (*Einleitung*), 1933. He gave an outline of the contents of the Introduction in the foreword to the commentary.

Gunkel made a major contribution to the study and classification of the types (*Gattungen*) of the Psalms. He was not the first to work on the psalm types, and acknowledged the studies of his predecessors in the area, for example, E. Reuss, F. Buhl, F. Baethgen, E. Kautzsch, E. König. But he was the first to classify and describe in detail all the psalm types of the Bible. He insisted that the study must include all the psalm material in the Bible, not only that in the Psalter, as well as the psalms and hymns in the deutero-canonical books and in the intertestamental literature. The task of psalm study is not merely to explain the individual psalms or the Psalter itself; its ultimate goal must be to describe the poetic style as a whole and its long and complicated history. The history of the psalms is the history of their literary forms (see above).

Israel's psalms, like Israel's stories (see above), had their origin in the life of the people. The people sang when Yahweh gave them victory (Exod 15:1, 21), when the ark was moved (Num 10:35), and when they walked to God's house (Ps 24:7-10; 42:5[4]; 95:1-7a; 100). The type must be distinguished according to the different circumstances in life. Psalms were first sung at worship. The basic cry was short and sharp: "Hallelujah," "Praise Yah(weh)." Only those psalms are to be brought together under one type, 1) which belong to a particular situation in the cult, 2) which share a common store of ideas and attitudes, and 3) whose elements have a common form of speech. The material, or content, and the form go together and must not be separated. Gunkel quoted Goethe with approval: "The material at hand (*Stoff*), everyone sees; the content (*Gehalt*), only the one who attends closely to it; the form (*Form*) remains a mystery to most" (*Einleitung*, p. 23).

Gunkel classified the psalms as: 1) hymns; 2) songs of the enthronement of Yahweh; 3) community laments; 4) royal psalms; 5) laments of the individual; 6) thanksgiving songs of the individual; 7) lesser types: a) pronouncements of curse and blessing, b) pilgrim songs, c) the victory song, d) Israel's thanksgiving song, e) the legend, f) the torah. He analyzed and described the structure and development of each of these types. At the same time, he gave careful attention to the prophetic elements in the psalms and to the relationship between the psalms and classical prophecy.

Gunkel's study led him to the conclusion that the hymn reached the fullness of its form and the high point of its development in the pre-exilic period. The form of the lament too was well established in the same period. The important elements and structure of both the hymn and the lament, therefore, were at hand to the classical prophets. The royal psalms and the enthronement psalms are only comprehensible under an existing monarchy.

The psalms originally came out of the cult. Gradually, pious people learned to sing hymns in which they stood detached from any external action. These hymns were no longer destined for public worship. At the same time there was a rebirth of the strong individualism of the prophets; people approached God alone. Thus arose the "spiritual poem" (*geistliche Dichtung*), which makes up a large part of the Psalter and remains its imperishable treasure, however inferior its poetry to that of the psalms of the cult (*Einleitung*, p. 30). The form remained traditional.

Collections of psalms were made at the close of the period of psalmic poetry and gave rise to the Psalter. But the process of collection contributed little to the understanding of the individual psalms. When the collections were at hand, public worship took possession of them, and the psalms were used as hymns in the temple. The circle from cult to cult was closed.

INDEX OF SUBJECTS

(Only pages 1 - 119 are indexed)

Abel 10, 15, 25, 33
     36, 38, 40, 48, 68, 73, 80, 96
Abimelech 15, 20, 24
     45, 56, 59-60, 75, 80, 85
Abraham/Abram 3, 6-7, 9, 13-6
     19-20, 22-5, 31-3, 36-40, 42-50, 52-3
     5-60, 64, 67, 69, 71-3, 75, 80-7, 89-92
     5-7, 99-102, 105-6, 110-2, 114, 116-7
Absalom 6
accommodation 73
Adah 76
Adam 30, 35-6, 39, 42-8, 51, 64, 70, 111
Adamah 72
Ahuzzath 76
Ammon 13-4, 32, 88
amplified style — see detailed
ancestors/ancestresses — see
  patriarchs, cult of the dead,
  eponyms
angel marriages (see also begetting)
     9-10, 63, 76, 78
angel(s) 5-6, 37, 78-9, 101, 112
anthropomorphisms — see God
apocalypse/apocalyptic 10, 31
apostles 2
Arab(s) 13, 30, 70, 76
Arabia(n) 63, 69
Aramaean(s) 14, 89, 97, 103
Ararat 5, 66
ark 5-6, 10, 42, 51-2, 73
Asher 89
Ashur 89, 102-4
Assyria(n) 66, 102, 104, 106
Baal 68
Babel 5, 20-1, 65, 78
Babel, tower of 9-11, 13
     32-3, 36, 39, 55, 65-6
Babylon 13, 55, 63-5
Babylonia(n) 65-6, 69, 71
     73, 78, 81, 90, 102, 115-6
Babylonian creation hymn 23
Babylonian creation story ... 11, 30, 113
Babylonian flood story 7, 11
Babylonian New Year feast 23

Babylonian New Year hymn 30
Babylonian documents 4-5
Baucis 69
Bedouin 15, 17, 69, 76
Beer-sheba 15, 18-20
     22, 24, 32, 65, 72, 74, 97, 101
begetting of gods (see also angel
  marriages) 11
Benjamin 36, 43, 59, 61-2, 72, 84
Bethel 19, 22, 24, 30, 32-3, 62, 65
     67-8, 72-3, 75, 79-80, 96, 110, 113
Bethharan 89
Bethuel 76
Bilhah 114
blessing, Isaac's (see also deception)
     76, 80, 114
blessings, a literary type 19, 28, 47
blessings of Jacob 28, 51, 97
Cain 10, 14-9, 21, 25, 33, 36, 38-40
     45-6, 48, 63-4, 68, 73, 81, 88, 96
Cainite 96
Calah 104
Canaan(ite) 9-10, 14-9, 32, 35, 39-40
     42, 52, 59, 64, 66-9, 72-3, 76, 78, 83
     8-9, 100, 102-3, 116
Canaanite civilization 66
Canaanite god 68
Canaanites 3, 15, 69
cattle breeders 66
character development 40, 42-7, 61
characters, number of 35-8
characters, secondary 38
characters, simplicity of 40-1
childbirth 12
Christmas 23
circumcision 22, 111-2, 116
context, lost in transmission 76
context, secondary to individuality ... 33
context, speeches vital to 46-7
convergence of traditions 72-3
Covenant Code 61
covenant (see also God-promise)
     82-3, 110-1, 113
creation 4-7, 10, 12, 22-3, 70, 111

creation, and spring 12
creation myth 71-2, 78
creation narrative(s)/story(ies) (see also
    Eden, primeval) 5, 7, 9, 11-2
    29, 36, 53, 57-8, 65-6, 71-2, 110, 113
creator 9
cult of the dead 90
cult stories 22, 29-31, 33, 79-80, 97, 103
cultic motifs 21-4
cycles of stories (see also Joseph,
    Jacob) 31-3, 40-1, 57-9, 92, 95-6
Dan 68
Daniel 75
David 3, 103
Dead Sea 5, 23, 30, 71
Deborah 62
deception of Isaac 19, 32-3, 36-7
    41, 51, 80, 87, 96, 100
detailed narratives 33, 48
    62, 95, 102, 110
deuteronomic reformation 80
deuteronomistic language 107
dietary laws 22, 24
Dinah 15, 17, 25-6, 36, 38, 67, 95
divine judgments 9
dreams 33, 41, 51, 60, 64, 75, 101
Dusares 90
E 17, 57, 65, 74-5, 79, 85-6, 93-8
    100-1, 105-7, 109, 112-5, 117
Easter 23
Eden / garden story 6, 9-13
    29-30, 32-3, 35-7, 39, 42, 46-8, 51, 57
    64, 66, 69, 72, 78
Edom 3, 14, 17, 25, 71-2, 88-9, 103
Egypt(ian) 4-5, 13, 16, 18, 25, 33
    36, 38-40, 45, 48, 50-2, 58-61, 63-4
    67, 69, 71, 76, 80, 82-4, 87-8, 97
    100, 102-4
Egyptian documents 4-5
Egyptian influence 67
Egyptians 70, 76, 111
El (see also Jacob-El, Joseph-El) 65
    68, 87
El-bethel 65
El-'elyon 65
El-'olam 65
El-roi 65
El-shaddai 65, 111-2

Elim 71
Elohim 100, 111
En-men-dur-Anna 66, 71
Enoch 66, 71
Ephraim 15, 72, 103
Ephrath 62, 67
epithets, absent in Genesis 56
eponyms 5, 13-5, 17, 89
Er 15, 25, 39
Esau 14-7, 24-5, 31, 33, 36-42, 45
    52, 54, 56-9, 66, 69, 71-3, 85, 88, 92
    95, 97, 100, 103, 114
Esther legend 23
esthetic taste/sense 7, 27
    34-6, 41, 74, 86, 91
ethnography(phic) 18-9, 24-5
ethnology(gical) 18-9, 24
etiology(gical) 12-3, 18-26, 80, 87
etymology(gical) ...5, 19-21, 24, 54-5, 66
Euphrates 5
Eve ... 5, 30, 35-7, 39, 42-8, 51, 64, 66, 70
exile 115-6
exodus story 23, 57, 59, 93
exodus 5, 118
Ezra 116-7
fairy tales 28, 52
family god 9, 77
family tree — see genealogy
farmer(s) 40, 64, 77, 86
Fear of Isaac 90
feasts — see festival
festival(s) (see also Passover,
    Purim, etc.) 23, 30
flood 78
flood narrative(s) / story(ies) 4, 7
    9-12, 29, 32-3, 36, 46, 54, 58, 66, 71
    78, 81-2, 105, 110, 112
folk narrative 56
folk tales 26, 52, 91
foreign gods 3, 74, 105
frame narratives 58-9, 117
Gad 89
garden of Eden — see Eden
genealogy 4, 13-4
    69, 73, 96, 99, 102, 109-11, 115-7
geological motifs 23
giants — see nᵉpilîm
Gerar 15, 18, 25, 42, 46, 64, 72, 75-6, 97

Gibeah 72
Gideon 82
Gilead 18-9, 72, 96
God (see also covenant) . . . . passim
God, afraid of humans 10, 64
God, anthropomorphisms 6, 10, 66, 78
God, as actor in stories 9-10
God, as judge 9
God, as universal creator 9
God, curses 19, 23, 35, 37, 45-6, 64
God, fidelity of 82
God, grace of 7, 9, 81, 86
God, mercy of 53, 81, 84, 86
God, oracles of 19
God, promise to Abraham 19, 33
                                        46, 56, 81-3
God, relationship to humans 80-3
God, revelation 6, 9, 22, 78-9, 101, 111-3
God, speaking 6, 46-7
God, theophanies 6, 10, 22-3, 32-3
           65, 73, 78-80, 87-8, 101, 110, 112-3
God, topic of narratives 6
God, working in history 6
gods — see Baal, begetting, Canaanite,
    Fear of Isaac, foreign, Gad, lᵉbana,
    Marduk, names, national, struggles,
    tarḫu
golden calf 105
Gomorrah 72
Greek(s) 13, 66, 69-71, 117-8
Greek parallels .69
Hagar .15, 24, 31
    33, 36-9, 42-8, 50-1, 53-5, 57, 76
    79-82, 84-5, 87, 95, 97, 111
Ham 15, 17, 63, 88, 103
Hammurapi 88, 104
Hamor 88
Haran 16, 64, 77, 89, 98
heaven(s) 4-6, 9-10
                        12, 23, 70, 79, 90, 101
heavenly council/court 4, 47, 90
Hebrew, language, age of 5
Hebron 10, 22, 24-5, 32-3, 36, 39
    44, 55, 57-8, 65, 67, 70-2, 75, 79-80
    82, 90, 95, 99, 101
Hirah 15, 39
historical narratives 29
history, and story 1-6

history, differences from story 2, 7
history, nature of 2
history, subject matter of 3
history, writing 1-2, 6-7, 62, 115
history of religion 22-3, 77, 102, 112
history of story 29
Hittites 103
Horite 76
hunter(s) 15-6, 40-1, 73, 76-7, 92
Hyksos 90
Hyrieus of Tanagra 69
immigration 14, 32, 39-40, 102
Indians 70
Iphigenia 69
Isaac (see also blessing, deception)
    9, 14-6, 19-22, 24-5, 31-3, 37, 40-2
    44-7, 49, 51, 53-6, 59, 61, 67, 69
    71-3, 76-7, 80, 83, 89-91, 97, 100
    102, 114
Iscah 76
Ishmael 14, 16-8, 23-4, 33, 37, 42
    46, 53-5, 63, 65, 69, 72-4, 80, 82, 85
    88, 97, 101, 111, 114
Ishmaelites 69, 95, 100
Israel (see also religion) . . . . passim
Israel, age of 4
Israel, as the people of God 9, 85, 94
Israel, as the name of Jacob 13
                            72, 88-9, 92, 100
Israel, racial purity of 14, 116
Israelite monarchy 17, 103
J 5, 17, 57, 65, 72, 74, 78, 85, 93-8
    100-1, 105-7, 109, 111-5, 117
Jabal 73
Jabneh 88
Jacob cycle 57, 59, 97
Jacob (see also blessing, Israel) 3, 9
    14-7, 19-20, 22-5, 28, 31-3, 36-42, 45
    47, 51-4, 56-9, 61-5, 67, 69, 71-5, 77
    79-85, 87-93, 95-7, 100-3, 105-6, 110
    114
Jacob, prayer of 81, 85
Jacob-El 65, 88
Japheth . . . 15-8, 35-6, 39-40, 43-4, 63, 88
Jaqubum 88
Jehovist 93, 106
Jephthah 88
Jerahmeel 88

Jericho 68
Jeruel 22, 54-5
Jerusalem 68, 80, 103, 112-3, 115
Jesus 2, 31
Jeush 89
Jezreel 88
Jonah 2
Jordan 21
Jordan valley 46
Joseph cycle/narratives/story 16
    33-4, 36-7, 40, 48, 57-9, 61, 64, 69-70
    73, 87, 90, 93, 95-7, 101-3
Joseph 18, 31, 33-4, 36, 38-41, 43
    45-6, 51-2, 57-61, 64, 67, 69-75, 79
    81, 84, 87, 89-90, 92-3, 95-7, 100-1
    103, 114
Joseph-El 65
Joshua 69, 75, 106
Josiah 107
Josiah, reform of 113
journey, as transition 58-9
Judah, person 15, 25, 36, 39, 45
    67, 76, 84, 96, 101-2
Judah, tribe of 15, 18, 25, 56, 71, 103
judges, period of 17-8, 102
Kemuel 76
Kenites 13, 73
Keturah 76
Laban 14, 16-7, 24-5, 31, 33, 38
    40, 42-3, 45, 47, 52, 56, 58, 62, 72-3
    3-4, 87, 89, 95, 97, 103, 105
Lahai-roi 22-4, 65, 72
lambs 20, 24
Lamech 69
language, origin of 12
laws of folk narrative 36-7
    40, 43, 49-50, 56, 60
Leah 3, 15, 39-42
legend 56, 83
Levi 14-5, 17, 63, 67, 71, 85
linguistics, origin of 19
linking passages 32, 58, 93
Lot 6, 13-4, 17-20, 23, 25, 31-2
    36, 38-40, 42, 44, 46, 48, 53, 57-9, 69
    73, 75, 81, 83-4, 95-6, 114
Lot's daughters 25, 44, 47, 60, 70, 84
Lot's wife 23
love, human 12, 41-4, 73, 95

lᵉbana (moon god) 89
Machpelah 62, 80, 97, 110
Mahanaim 54, 62, 65, 72, 80
Manasseh 15, 72, 103
Marduk 30
maṣṣēḇōt / memorial stones 22
    80, 105, 113
Mesopotamia 66
messenger of God/Yahweh (see also
    angel) 79, 87
meter (see also rhythm) 27-9
Methuselah 89
metric pattern 28
Midianites .96, 100
midrashic legend 117
migration 16, 25
    59, 67-9, 73, 75, 82-3, 97
Milcah 76, 89
Moab 13-4, 32, 69, 88
monarchy — see Israelite
monologue (see also speeches) 47
monotheism 11, 78
months, numbering of 116
moon god (lᵉbana) 89
morality 57, 63, 74, 83-6, 105, 112-3, 118
Mosaic law 111
Moses 1, 22-3, 59
    69, 74, 96, 100, 105, 109-12, 118
motifs (see also cultic ethnography,
    ethnology, etiology, etymology,
    geological) 18-26
motifs, anticipatory 52
motifs, elaboration of 99
motifs, mingling of   24-5, 55-6, 82-3, 114
motifs, running through a story . . 51, 60
motifs, secular and religious 82
myth, and patriarchs 11, 90-1
myth, and story 10-1
myth, as teaching 12
myth, definition of 10, 12
myth, difference from story 10, 57
myth, OT hostility toward 11, 78
myths, Babylonian 11
Nabataean 90
Nahor 16, 49, 64, 76, 89
names in Genesis (see also
    etymology) 5, 17
names 88, 104

names, double 17
names, Egyptian 104
names, of God 65, 71, 90
names, of patriarchs 88-90
names, Israelite 67
names, word plays on 54
narrative(s) — see story, creation,
    detailed, frame, flood, folk,
    historical, laws, linking, poetic,
    primal, spiritual
narrative style 3, 28, 50, 56-62
narrative style, different from
    modern 48
national god 77
naḥar 89
Negev 101
nᵉp̄ilîm 51, 78
New Testament 2, 93
New Year — see Babylonian
Nile 48
Nimrod 66, 76
Nineveh 103-4
Noah . . . 4-6, 10, 32-3, 35, 37, 42, 46, 48-9
    54, 57, 64, 66, 71-2, 76, 81-2, 111
nomads 68
notes 53, 62
    67, 75, 82, 97, 99, 102, 110, 114
novelette 61-2, 67
Novella 62
numen (numina) 9, 64, 71, 77
nābî' — see prophets
Obed-edom 89
Onan 15, 25, 81
Ophrah 68
oral tradition 2-4, 29-31
    63, 74, 93, 98-9, 118
oral transmission 3, 44
P   58, 65, 72, 75, 94, 97, 102, 106, 109-17
P, style of 109-11, 113, 115
Paddan 97
pagan(ism) 66, 86, 106, 112-3
pagans 116
Palestine 5
paradise — see Eden
parallelism 28
Passover 21, 23

patriarch(s) (see also myth) 3, 9
    13, 19, 23, 63-8, 72-3, 77, 79-80, 82-5
    89-92, 96, 100, 105, 110, 112-3, 116
patriarch(s), as gods 89-91
patriarch(s), historicity of 14-6, 91-2
patriarchal narratives/stories 3-5
    9-11, 13-7, 26, 38, 47, 59, 66-9, 73
    82-4, 86, 88, 93, 102-3, 109, 111, 113
patriarchal period 3-4
Pentateuch (see also Torah,
    Samaritan) 31, 117-8
Penuel 10, 22-5, 33, 36, 39, 54, 64-5
    71-3, 77, 79-80, 95
Perez 15, 25
Persians 70
Pharaoh   33, 36, 38, 40, 46, 50, 84-5, 100
Phicol 76
Philemon 69
Philistine 3
Philistines 3, 76, 96, 103
Philo 66
philosophy, origin of 12
philosophy of history, origin of 19
Phoenician 66
poetic narrative 2
poetry 2, 4, 7, 18, 27-8, 61, 110
poetry, and myth 11
poetry, and story 7-8
polytheism 65, 71, 75, 112
popular tradition 1-3, 14, 16, 29
    31, 53, 62, 74, 93, 106
postbiblical period 12
Potiphar 100
Potiphar's wife 25, 33, 69-70
prayer of Jacob 81, 85
Priestly Code — see P
primal narratives/stories . . . 26, 58-9, 91
primeval history 98
primeval sea 51, 66
primeval stories 9-13, 34, 64-7, 69
    78, 86, 93, 96-7, 100, 109
prolixity 33-4, 59, 61, 109-10
promise — see covenant, God
prophecy 72, 104-6
prophets   6, 10, 28, 51, 56, 80, 105-6, 113
Purim 23

Rabbis 118
Rachel 3, 15, 25, 39-40, 62, 74, 84, 89, 96
rainbow 12, 111
ram 22
Ramses II 89
rationalism 21
Rebekah 15-6, 33, 36-8, 40-1, 44
        46-9, 59, 62, 74-5, 79, 81, 87, 98
redactors 74, 77, 99, 106-7, 117
Reformation, Protestant 21
religion and story 6
religion of Israel 2, 23, 77-9, 81, 119
religion of Israel, and myth 11
religion of Israel, and poetry 2
Reuben, tribe of 15
Reuben 15, 17-8, 21, 36, 63, 67, 69
                71, 76, 85, 96, 101-2
rhythm (see also meter) 27-9
righteousness 81, 85-6
romance, a literary type 29, 62
r°'u 89
Sabaean 89
sabbath 12, 22, 111-2, 116
sacrifice 6-7, 10, 25, 31, 46, 54, 69
                83, 105, 112, 116
sacrifice of Isaac 7, 25
        31-2, 36, 40, 42, 45-6, 49, 53-4, 59
        61, 80-1, 83, 87, 95, 101
Samaritan Pentateuch 117
Samaritan schism 117
Samson 2, 82
sanctuaries (see also temples, cultic)
        20, 22-3, 29-31, 72, 80, 103, 105, 113
Sarah (Sarai) .. 15, 24, 33, 37-9, 43, 45-8
        50, 52, 62, 75, 82, 84-5, 89, 111, 117
Saul 103
scene, repetition of 59-60
scenes 34-5, 37, 55, 59-60, 86
science, origin of 18
Septuagint 118
Sethite 96
Seti I 89
Se'ir 71
Shamshi Adad I 104
Shaul 76
Shechem 3, 14-5, 17-8, 22, 25, 36
        62, 67-8, 72, 74-5, 86, 88, 102
sheep breeders 17, 68, 84

Shelah 25
Shem 15-7, 35-6, 39-40, 43-4, 63, 88, 111
shepherd(s) 15-6
        40-1, 64, 73, 77, 80, 86, 92
Shiloh 68
shrines — see sanctuaries
Shua 15
Simeon 14-5, 17, 63, 67, 71, 85
snake 5-6, 12, 35, 37, 39, 42, 45-7, 52
Sodom 10, 23-5, 30, 32, 36, 43, 57-8
        60, 64, 69-70, 72, 81, 97, 99, 106
Sodomites 40
Solomon 103
sons of the east 16, 18
sons of patriarchs — see mother's or
        father's name
sorcerer 71
source criticism (see also E, J, P,
        vocabulary) 51, 94-8, 100-2, 116
speeches (see also monologue) 45-7
        49-50, 59-61, 75, 84-5, 106
spiritual narrative 83
story (see also creation, cycles, flood,
        Joseph, narrative, primal,
        primeval) .... passim
story, age of 17-8, 34
        63, 87-8, 95-6, 101-2, 106-7
story, as poetry 27-9
story, believability of 4-6, 8
story, conclusions/climax 49
story, details in 48-9
story, foreign influences 65-9, 71-2
story, foreign parallels 69-71
story, history (of transmission) ... 17, 29
        69, 71-7, 83, 87-8, 93-7, 99, 106
story, length of 33-5, 57, 59, 61
story, nature of 2
story, plot/action 49-50, 57
story, subject matter of 3
story, taxonomy of 18-9, 24
story, transitions between 58, 62
story, units in 31-3
story, written down 93, 104-7
storyteller(s) 30, 34-5, 38, 42-61
        67, 72, 74-7, 86, 91, 93, 98, 115
struggles between the gods 11
style of Genesis 27-9
styles, age of 62

Succoth 67
Syria(n) 66, 73, 89
Syro-Canaanite 71
table of the nations 5, 100, 103
Tamar 15, 25-6
   43, 45, 56, 67, 76, 84, 97, 101
tarḫu (Syrian god) 89
tax, Egyptian 18
Tell El-Amarna 66
temple (see also sanctuaries) 80
   89, 112, 116
Terah 89
teraphim 105
theocracy 112
theology, origin of 12
theophanies — see God
Thutmose III 88-9
Tigris 5, 102
Timnah 36
tithe 22
Torah 93, 118
tower — see Babel
transition — see linking, journey
treaty 15, 18, 24-5, 72, 74-5, 96
tree(s), cultic 22-3, 64, 79
tree, of knowledge 5, 42, 47

tree, of life 5
trial (legal) 35
tribes — see individual names
tribes, twelve 13-6, 33, 102
Tubal 73
universalistic attitude/ideas 66, 78
Ur 16, 97
Usoos 66
variants 3, 29
   55, 60, 74-5, 78, 83-4, 95, 100, 107
vocabulary of sources 96, 100
wife, passed as sister 25, 46, 50, 85-6
worship 21-2, 80, 105, 112
writing — see story-written
writing, fixes tradition 3
Yahweh 9, 17, 21, 23, 57, 65, 71, 78
   82, 84, 86-7, 94, 96, 100, 105, 111-2
Yahweh ṣᵉbā'ôṯ 65
Yahweh's messenger (see also angel,
   messenger) 87
Zeboiim 72
Zerah 15, 25
Zilpah 114
Zipporah 74
Zoar 20, 23, 72

INDEX OF SCRIPTURE CITATIONS

(Only pages 1 - 119 are indexed)

GENESIS

Chapter 1 ... 4, 7, 47, 53, 66, 109, 111
1:6ff 5
1:26 47
1:28ff 110
1:29-30 111
Chapter 2 46
Chapters 2-3 57
2:2-3 22
2:4 9
2:5ff 9
2:10-14 5
2:14 102
2:16-17 47
2:17 42
2:18 .... 4, 47
2:19-20 6
2:24 12
2:25 43-4
Chapter 3 .... 35, 45
3:1ff 45-6
3:5 37
3:6 42
3:7 43-5
3:9ff 47
3:14ff 37, 46
3:16ff 45
3:22 47
4:1 .... 21, 42
4:5 42
4:6ff 47
4:8 .... 45, 48
4:11-12 47
4:13ff 46
4:17ff 77
4:19 76
Chapter 5 110-1
5:27 5
5:29 96
6:1-4 10
6:1ff 5, 10, 63, 76, 78
6:3 4
6:4 78
6:6-7 4

6:7 .... 47, 117
7:1ff 47
7:3 117
7:7 .... 42, 117
7:8-9 117
7:16 6
7:22-23 117
8:4 54
8:7 99
8:8 42
8:9 54
8:11 76
8:21 .... 6, 54
8:21-22 ....12, 47
8:22 66
9:1ff 110
9:3ff 111
9:8ff 12
9:12ff 12
9:18-19 5
9:20-21 48
9:20ff 15, 35, 39, 49
9:22 75
9:23 .... 36, 43
9:24 42
9:24ff 18, 37
9:25ff 19, 47
Chapter 10 110
10:8-19 5
10:9 76
10:11 103
10:11-12 104
10:16-18 107
10:21 5
10:24 117
10:25-30 5
Chapter 11 32
11:5 64
11:6 64
11:6-7 ....4, 47
11:7 47
11:9 20
11:10ff 110-1
11:11 109

GENESIS 11:29 76
Chapter 12 . . . . 39, 42, 74, 83, 87, 106
12:1ff 95
12:2 47
12:2-3 19
12:6 . . . . 3, 22
12:6-8 67
12:7 . . . . 19, 47
12:10ff . . .16, 36, 38, 40, 50, 76, 82, 85
12:11ff 46
12:15 36
12:17 75
12:17ff 86
12:18-19 85
12:20 . . . . 84, 99
Chapter 13 . . . . 19, 36, 83
13:2ff 39
13:5ff 67
13:7 3
13:7ff 38
13:14-17 . . . . .61, 83, 107
13:14ff 47, 75, 81
13:18ff 46
Chapter 14 3
14:3 5
14:14-15 5
Chapter 15 . . . . 47, 65
                            75, 81-3, 87, 95, 106
15:3 77
15:7-8 117
15:15 117
15:17 6
15:18 19
15:19-21 107
Chapter 16 . . . . 18, 24
    31, 33, 36, 38-9, 46, 50, 57, 74
    76, 80, 82, 84-5, 87, 95, 97, 101
16:4 52
16:4-5 48
16:5 . . . . 64, 87
16:6 . . . . 43, 45, 52
16:7 79
16:7ff 23, 86
16:8 47
16:8ff 47
16:9-10 . . . . .61, 107
16:11ff 54
16:13 . . . . 65, 71

16:14 . . . . 72, 75
Chapter 17 . . . . 110, 112
17:9ff 110-1
17:17 112
Chapter 18   33, 39, 57, 78, 80-2, 101
Chapters 18-19 . . . . .6, 10
18:1ff 23
18:2ff 43-4
18:4 22
18:6ff 48
18:8 79
18:10 . . . . 46, 99
18:12 . . . . 21, 47
18:12ff 24
18:16 58
18:17-19 . . . . .61, 107
18:17ff 47, 75
18:20-21 43
18:21 64
18:23-33 61
18:23ff 60, 75, 99, 106
Chapter 19 . . . . 23, 32, 57, 78, 101
19:8 28
19:14 . . . . 36, 42
19:17ff 23, 75
19:20 20
19:20-23 72
19:22 20
19:26 23
19:27-28 . . . . .43, 58
19:30 69
19:30ff 36
19:31 47
19:32 44
19:38 3
Chapter 20 . . . . .56, 59-60
                            72, 74, 76, 83, 97
20:3 79
20:7 . . . . 80, 105
20:9 45
20:12 . . . . 84, 86
20:15 84
20:16 84
20:18 107
Chapter 21 . . . . 77, 80-1, 87, 95
21:3 101
21:4ff 37

GENESIS 21:6 42
21:8ff 33, 74, 82, 84, 97, 101
21:10 47
21:11-13 85
21:11ff 75, 84
21:14 . . . . 45, 72, 85
21:17 . . . . 53, 79, 101
21:17ff 86
21:18 42
21:19 44
21:22ff 15, 18, 24, 76, 97
21:24 47
21:28ff 20, 24
21:32 . . . . 96, 101
21:33 . . . . 65, 71
21:34 96
Chapter 22   22, 31-3, 36, 40, 42, 46
              49, 54, 80-1, 83, 87, 95, 101
22:3 43
22:4ff 49
22:7-8 . . . . .45, 55
22:8 53-4
22:9 45
22:9-10 60
22:11 6
22:11ff 86
22:12 54
22:13 54
22:14 54
22:15-18 107
22:15ff 75
22:19 22
22:20ff 99
22:21 76
Chapter 23 110
23:17 109
23:18 109
Chapter 24 . . . . 31, 33
              37-8, 40, 49, 59, 81, 95
24:10-11 16
24:18-19 47
24:30-31 43
24:50 64
24:61ff 87
24:65 44
24:67 42
25:1 76
25:1ff 99

25:9 114
25:11 72
25:12ff 110
25:24ff 42
25:25 41
25:26 20
25:29ff 36
25:33 47
Chapter 26 . . . . 15, 24
              72, 74, 76, 83, 96
26:3 107
26:7 . . . . 42, 47
26:12ff 84
26:22-23 64
26:23ff 72
26:24 107
26:25 107
26:25ff 18-9
26:26 76
26:32 47
26:34ff 114
Chapter 27 . . . . .19, 32, 37-8, 40-1, 47
              51, 87, 96, 100, 103
27:4 76
27:15 77
27:28 77
27:28ff 19
27:33 42
27:36 . . . . 45, 85
27:38 76
27:40 . . . . 72, 103
27:42ff 58
27:43 98
27:46 117
28:1-9 116
28:1ff 114
28:4 114
28:10 98
28:10ff 23-4, 33, 67
28:13 19
28:13-14 47
28:14 107
28:17 42
28:18 . . . . 22, 80
28:19 72
28:21 107
28:22 . . . . 22, 105
28:31 77

GENESIS 29:1ff 74
29:4 98
29:14 47
29:17 41
29:18 42
29:31 81
29:31ff 39, 93
29:32 21
29:35 42
30:1 42
30:2 42
30:14 95
30:17 95
30:25ff 77, 80
31:3 83
31:4ff 84
31:7 84
31:13 . . . . 65, 71
31:23ff 38
31:26ff 56
31:30ff 105
31:33ff 87
31:34 84
31:36 42
31:36ff 84
31:42 90
31:43 45
31:49ff 107
31:52 . . . . 18-9, 72, 96
32:1ff 80
32:2-3 62
32:4ff 52, 72
32:7 38
32:8 42
32:9 . . . . 42, 45
32:10-13 . . . . .81, 107
32:10-18 107
32:10ff 85
32:21 42
32:23ff 24, 36
32:25ff 10, 33, 39, 79-80
32:27 53
32:31-32 72
32:33 22
33:17 77
33:17ff 67
33:18 72
33:18ff 62

Chapter 34 . . . . 15, 17, 25, 3\
38, 67, 85, 102, 107, 117
34:3 42
34:7 . . . . 42, 87
35:1ff 67
35:2ff 75
35:4 105
35:6 110
35:8 62
35:11ff 110
35:13-14 117
35:14 62
35:16ff 62, 67
35:21-22 85
35:22 . . . . 67, 76
35:29 114
Chapter 36 . . . . 110, 117
36:2 76
36:24 76
36:31ff 3
Chapter 37 . . . . 41, 51, 58
37:2 114
37:3 42
37:4 42
37:8 . . . . 101, 103
37:9 90
37:24 45
37:25 95
37:28 . . . . 45, 96
37:35 95
Chapter 38 . . . . 15, 25
39, 43, 45, 67, 97, 102
38:7 64
38:9-10 81
38:10 64
38:11 76
38:21 36
38:25ff 86
38:27ff 15
Chapter 39 41
39:1 107
39:19 42
Chapter 40 41
Chapters 40-41 60
40:1 38
40:2 42
Chapter 41 . . . . 41, 75
41:1ff 86

GENESIS 41:37ff 52
41:45 104
41:50 107
42:1 58
42:6 . . . . 52, 58
42:13 61
42:21 . . . . 45, 61
42:24 43
42:25ff 60
42:30ff 61
Chapters 43-44 60
43:3 61
43:7 61
43:16ff 39
43:20-21 61
43:30 . . . . 43, 61
44:1ff 60
44:19ff 61
45:19 107
45:26ff 61
46:1 . . . . 101, 107
46:1-3 97
46:3 107
46:8-27 117
46:10 76
46:29ff 37
47:1 84
47:7-11 109
47:13ff 19, 33, 67, 97
47:29ff 96
47:31 . . . . 51, 87
Chapter 48 51
48:7 96
48:10 101
48:13-14 15
48:13ff 72, 103
48:22 . . . . 18, 72
Chapter 49 . . . . 19, 28, 97, 99
49:3-4 . . . . .15, 18, 102
49:3-7 85
49:11-12 77
49:15 77
49:20 77
49:27 84
49:33 51
Chapter 50 60
50:11 107
50:20 101

50:24 107

EXODUS
2:15ff 74
3:1ff 23
3:14 21
4:14ff 22
12:26 21
12:26-27 30
13:11-12 30
13:14 21
Chapter 32 105

DEUTERONOMY 61, 107

JOSHUA
Joshua 4:6 . . . . .21, 30
Chapter 24 106

JUDGES 17
Chapter 1 17
7:20 82
Chapter 19 72

SAMUEL 2, 39
1 Samuel 24:20 81
2 Samuel 6
3:39 81
Chapter 24 103

KINGS 2
2 Kings 23 80

ISAIAH
51:1-2 89
63:16 89

JEREMIAH 61
31:15 89

EZEKIEL 116

HOSEA 105

AMOS 61, 105-6

HAGGAI 116

ZECHARIAH 116

PSALMS 61

PROVERBS 61

JOB 65

DANIEL 2 75

EZRA 116

NEHEMIAH 116

CHRONICLES 116
2 Chronicles 20:16 54

SIRACH 44:19 84

INDEX OF MODERN AUTHORS

(Only pages 1 - 119 are indexed)

Bader, K. 62
Budde, K. 94
Dundes, A. 37
Eerdmans, B.D. 24, 90
Geldner, K.F. 28
Goethe, J.W. 52
Gressmann, H. 12, 26
        68, 77, 80, 88, 90-1, 102
Grimm, J. 20, 62
Haller, E. 82, 86
Hauff, W. 58
Lagarde, P.A. de 90, 104
Littmann, E. 28

Meyer, E. 26, 68, 88, 90, 100
Noldeke, T. 28
Olrik, A. 36, 38, 40
        43-4, 49-50, 52, 56-8, 60
Paulsen, F. 2
Ranke, H. 88
Sievers, E. 27-8
Spiegelberg, W. 104
Wellhausen, J. 17, 33
        94, 106, 109-10, 115-6
Wildeboer, G. 94
Winckler, H. 90
Wundt, W. 26

Other Titles Available from BIBAL Press

Balla	*The Four Centuries Between the Testaments*	$ 7.95
Christensen	*Prophecy and War in Ancient Israel*	14.95
Christensen	*Experiencing the Exodus from Egypt*	7.95
Clements	*Wisdom for a Changing World*	7.95
Elliott	*Seven-Color Greek Verb Chart*	3.50
Haïk-Vantoura	*The Music of the Bible Revealed*	29.95
Lohfink	*Option for the Poor*	7.95
Lohfink	*Opción por el Pobre*	7.95
Lohfink	*The Inerrancy of Scripture and Other Essays*	13.95
McKenzie	*Sacred Images and the Millennium*	7.50
Reid	*Enoch and Daniel*	12.95
Schneck	*Isaiah in the Gospel of Mark, I-VIII*	19.95
Scott	*A Simplified Guide to BHS*	6.95
Scott	*Guia para el Uso de la BHS*	6.95
Sinclair	*Jesus Christ According to Paul*	12.95
Sinclair	*Revelation: A Book for the Rest of Us*	12.95
St. Clair	*Prayers for People Like Me*	6.95
St. Clair	*Co-Discovery: The Theory and Practice of Experiential Theology*	12.95
Terpstra	*Life is to Grow On: The ABC's of Holistic Growth*	16.95

Prices subject to change

Postage & Handling: (for USA addresses) $2.00 for first copy + 50¢
for each additional copy

California residents add 7.25% sales tax

Write for a free catalog:
BIBAL Press
P. O. Box 4531
Vallejo, CA 94590